YORK NO

General Editors: Profe
of Stirling) & Professo
University of Beirut)

Robert Bolt

A MAN FOR
ALL SEASONS

Notes by Tony Bareham

MA (OXFORD) DPHIL (COLERAINE)
Senior Lecturer in English
The New University of Ulster

LONGMAN
YORK PRESS

YORK PRESS
Immeuble Esseily, Place Riad Solh, Beirut.

LONGMAN GROUP LIMITED
Longman House, Burnt Mill,
Harlow, Essex CM20 2JE, England
and Associated Companies throughout the World.

© Librairie du Liban 1980

First published 1980; reprinted 1983 and 1985
ISBN 0 582 78181 7
Produced by Longman Group (FE) Ltd
Printed in Hong Kong

Contents

Part 1

Introduction

The author

Robert Bolt was born in Manchester in 1924. He was educated at Manchester Grammar School, but left with few qualifications. After a spell in an insurance office, which he hated, he was offered a place at Manchester University, where he read history.

During the war Bolt served in the Air Force and Army, and then completed his degree. He also had a post-graduate year at Exeter University. His interest in history shows in *A Man For All Seasons*, where factual accuracy combines with imagination to make a good play.

As a young man Bolt was a member of the Communist Party, but later grew disillusioned with organised socialism and left it. He was once put in prison for deliberately breaking the law as a protest against the Atom Bomb. His concern with law and with civil disobedience shows in *A Man For All Seasons*.

For a while Bolt taught at Millfield School, where he was Head of the English Department. During this time he wrote a number of radio plays, and did some directing in the theatre. As a teacher he learned to hold people's interest. Theatre directing trained his eye for the practical side of drama—how to keep the story on the move, create lively and credible characters, and how to use the stage efficiently and effectively. In writing for radio he developed a good ear for dialogue.

The success of his first play, *Flowering Cherry* (1957), encouraged him to give up teaching and to become a full-time dramatist. Since then he has written several very successful plays. *A Man For All Seasons* is the best known, though *The Thwarting of Baron Bolligrew* (1965) is one of the liveliest plays for children written in the last twenty years, and *Vivat, Vivat Regina!* (1970) also had a long run on the stage in London.

Like many other modern playwrights Robert Bolt is also interested in the cinema. His film scripts include *Lawrence of Arabia* and *Doctor Zhivago*. His own adaptation of *A Man For All Seasons* was as popular in the cinema as it had been on stage.

Background to the play

A Man For All Seasons is set in the reign of King Henry VIII, which lasted from 1509 to 1547. Some knowledge of events during that time is necessary for understanding the plot in Bolt's play. He refers to a number of these, and sometimes actually uses the words spoken by the real-life characters, as in Act 2, Scene 8, at the trial of Sir Thomas More. Nearly all Bolt's characters are based on real people—only the Common Man and Chapuys's Attendant are not. He sometimes makes minor alterations, since the real Norfolk was less sympathetic than Bolt's character, and the real Rich was more ominous. Bolt's alterations tell us something about his intentions in *A Man For All Seasons*.

The House of Tudor

England had endured civil war from 1455 to 1485. One party—the Lancastrians—took as their badge the red rose, whilst their opponents —the Yorkists—chose the white rose. Hence this civil war was called the Wars of the Roses.

Eventually the Lancastrians were victorious, and their leader became King of England as Henry VII. Henry's family name was Tudor.

Henry VII had two sons, Arthur and Henry. To increase the popularity and power of Arthur a marriage was arranged for him with Catherine of Aragon. She came from Spain, which was the most powerful nation in Europe; an alliance between England and Spain, was, therefore, politically desirable.

Arthur died at the age of sixteen, before coming to the throne, and Henry became King in 1509, as Henry VIII. A marriage was arranged for him with Arthur's widow to retain the advantages of the Spanish alliance. Since the Catholic Church taught that it was illegal for a man to marry his brother's widow, this could only be done with the special permission of the Pope, through a dispensation.

Henry and Catherine had several children, but none of their sons lived beyond infancy. The Queen's failure to provide male heirs explains Henry's desire to divorce her.

The divorce

Only the Pope could break Henry's marriage, by giving him another dispensation. The divorce, however, insulted Spain. At this time the Spanish had sacked Rome, where the Pope lived, and he was virtually a prisoner of King Charles V. This made it unlikely that the Pope would do as Henry wished.

The matter grew even more urgent when Henry fell in love with Lady Anne Boleyn. Personal and political motives coincided to make King Henry drive his administrators to obtain the divorce. Wolsey was his chief negotiator.

Henry had persuaded himself that his marriage was sinful. The Book of Leviticus in the Old Testament of the Bible says: 'Thou shalt not uncover the nakedness of thy brother's wife: it is thy brother's nakedness . . .' and goes on to threaten that such marriages will produce no male heirs. Such had been Henry's case, so he could cite scripture to justify his desire for a divorce, though the issue was confused by another quotation which had formerly been used to allow the marriage. Deuteronomy 25:17 says

If brothers dwell together, and one of them dies and has no son, the wife of the dead shall not be married outside the family to a stranger; her husband's brother shall go in to her, and take her as his wife . . .

Hence the issue was extremely complex.

The Reformation

Up to this time there had been only one Christian church in Western Europe—the Roman Catholic Church. The Pope was its head, and he was ostensibly the spiritual and temporal overlord of all Christian nations. He could over-rule individual monarchs. But as some nations grew powerful they came to resent such interference in their affairs.

There were many things wrong with the Catholic Church. Sometimes a bad Pope was elected; evil practices had arisen, such as the granting of indulgences. In return for monetary payment the Church would grant forgiveness for sins. Sometimes the priests were lazy or ignorant. Many people wished for changes, but the only way to achieve them was to break from the Church of Rome, and establish new churches. Among the reformers was the German professor, Martin Luther (1483–1546), who is mentioned several times in *A Man For All Seasons*. Like all those who rebelled against the Pope he was termed a heretic, and was expelled, or excommunicated.

When the Pope refused Henry his divorce the King decided to break with the Church of Rome. By declaring himself head of his own national church, Henry could arrange the divorce for himself. His selfish wishes and a genuine desire for change thus coincided to bring about the Reformation which gave birth to the Church of England.

The Act of Supremacy

To establish his new church Henry had to change the law. He persuaded Parliament to pass the Act of Supremacy. This stated that the King was 'Protector and Only Supreme Head of the Church and Clergy in England'. The Act is mentioned in Bolt's play (p.48).

The English bishops did not dare to refuse the King, but they added to the new Act the words 'so far as the laws of Christ permit'. This made little difference to Henry, but More hoped for some protection from these words in his steadfast opposition to Henry's action. Since it was difficult to prove how far the law of God 'allowed' the King to be Supreme Head of his own Church, More hoped he might be able to continue serving under the new order of things, whilst retaining his private loyalty to the Pope in spiritual matters.

The Act of Succession

The Act of Succession (1534) declared that Anne's children, not Catherine's, should rule England after Henry's death. It was deemed treasonable to disagree with the new marriage, and influential people had to swear an oath to abide by the Act of Succession. It was after his refusal to take this oath that More was arrested.

The Renaissance

This term means, literally, 'the re-birth'. It refers to the renewal of interest in Greek and Latin literature and ideas. The New Learning is mentioned several times in *A Man For All Seasons*.

For men like More the Renaissance offered a liberalising influence, since many of the Greek philosophers had expressed truths which became lost in Europe before More's time. But the Greek writers were not Christians, and their ideas on government and civic responsibility were not always in accord with Catholic teaching. They believed that responsibility is an individual matter. Each man must act according to his own conscience. In the hands of unscrupulous and ambitious politicians such ideas can be dangerous.

Because the Renaissance stressed the responsibility of the individual it weakened the authority of the Pope and of the Catholic Church as the centre of power. This encouraged men like Cromwell to argue that 'administrative convenience' is more desirable than strict morality; whatever is good for the State must be done, whatever the Church might think. Bolt presents both viewpoints in this debate between conscience and central policy. The issue is as relevant today as it was in the time of More.

The Council

In Henry's reign the Council was more powerful than Parliament. It comprised the nobility selected to advise the King, with a few commoners who were experts on such matters as finance and law. Since Councillors were picked by the King he usually had his way regardless of popular feeling in the country.

A note on the text

Robert Bolt's *A Man For All Seasons*, was published in the Heinemann Drama Library series, Heinemann Educational Books, London, 1961, and in French's Acting Edition, Samuel French & Co, Ltd., London, 1961. This edition has two photographs of the original production, and a stage-plan.

The text has subsequently been published by Random House, Toronto, 1962, and by Bellhaven Books, Toronto, 1963. The latter edition has notes and questions on the play. *A Man For All Seasons* has also been published in the Hereford Plays series, edited by E.R. Wood, Heinemann Educational Books, London, 1963. This is the edition used for these Notes. It has its own notes by E.R. Wood, which will be found a helpful supplement to those provided here. There have been fourteen re-prints of this edition. The text has also been published by Vintage Books, New York, 1965.

Part 2

Summaries

of A MAN FOR ALL SEASONS

A general summary

At the beginning of the play Sir Thomas More appears a contented and prosperous man. He is giving a party for friends, and the atmosphere is relaxed. There are, however, clouds on his horizon. Rich, a young acquaintance of his, pesters him for a job, which More refuses to arrange for him since he feels Rich lacks integrity. There is much dislike and fear of Thomas Cromwell, who is growing in political power. Cromwell represents a new way of life in which political necessity dominates individual conscience.

More is summoned to discuss the King's divorce with Cardinal Wolsey, who makes clear the King's insistence upon matters going as he wishes. More's general popularity makes his assistance highly desirable. Though he deftly evades Wolsey's demands, the problem is shelved not solved.

Cromwell and Chapuys, the Spanish Ambassador, are working to ascertain More's opinions and intentions. William Roper, a London lawyer, wishes to marry More's daughter, but is refused permission since his religious opinions are heretical.

When Wolsey dies More is made Chancellor. Cromwell and Chapuys increase their efforts to make More speak his mind on the divorce.

King Henry visits More, ostensibly for a friendly dinner party, but in reality to persuade the Chancellor to help him. More regretfully refuses, and the King leaves in anger. Meanwhile Cromwell bullies and bribes the discontented Rich into helping him to coerce More to accept the divorce. The first Act ends at this crucial stage.

Two years have passed when Act 2 opens. Henry now has his divorce. More resigns as Chancellor, asking only to be left in peace without being made to give a public statement of his opinions. Henry is insistent on More's approval, since More's popularity will lead other people to believe as he does.

The Duke of Norfolk is frightened into helping Cromwell obtain a statement from More who, in his retirement, has become painfully poor. Hence he is urged both by the State and by his family to yield to the mounting pressures on him.

When the Act of Succession is passed More refuses to take the oath. He is imprisoned in The Tower and interrogated. A visit from his family fails to change his mind, and he is brought to trial on a charge of high treason. Cromwell bribes Rich to lie in court, and on his uncorroborated evidence More is sentenced to death.

Detailed summaries

The Preface

Paragraphs 1 & 2. Bolt reminds us that Henry VIII stood up against the full power of the Church, and brought about the collapse of a long-established way of life.

Paragraphs 3–12. There follows a description of the events leading up to Henry's desire for a divorce from Queen Catherine.

Paragraph 13. A new section of the argument begins here. So far it has seemed that the play must be concerned with religion, but nowadays we are more interested in sociology and economics.

Paragraphs 14 & 15. This interest in economics makes us see things as apparently inevitable. People become merely 'accidents'—they matter less than the trends and movements by which we now measure history and progress. Bolt believes that individuals matter more than theories.

Paragraphs 16–18. The argument about individuals in society is taken further. It is difficult to sense our individual importance so we turn to 'the professional describers'; to people who invent categories and types. We are empty people, like modern cities which are empty at night when everyone goes home from work. Life emphasises economics—'get and spend' becomes the purpose of our lives.

Paragraphs 19–21. Bolt chose More as his hero because More had a sense of himself as an individual; 'he knew where he began and left off'. He could have avoided death by taking the oath accepting Henry's divorce and re-marriage, but his refusal was part of his realisation of his 'selfhood'.

We may find it hard today to understand such a man. We no longer believe in ourselves in the same way, nor, Bolt feels, does western man set such store by the sanctity of giving his word on oath.

Paragraph 25. More is attractive because he managed to be successful in the world although he had such high ideals.

Paragraphs 26–28. Despite his enjoyment of a successful life, More believed himself a servant of the Church of Christ. He did not, however, seek martyrdom. Loss of his life was insignificant when balanced against loss of his immortal soul if he took an oath falsely. He fought hard to avoid his death, trusting in the law to defend him. But when Cromwell bribed Rich to commit perjury there was no law left. Cromwell did not just break the law, he chose to operate in a world where law no longer existed; he reduced society to chaos.

These paragraphs deal with the meaning of the play. The rest of the Preface discusses the way it is written.

Paragraph 29. The play employs numerous metaphors. The sea, rivers, and water represent 'the superhuman context', the unknown and unchanging forces which surround us. By contrast dry land is a metaphor of society, of the known laws and rules of everyday existence.

Paragraphs 30–34. The play is not realistic. Bolt took an historical theme and treated it in the manner of Bertold Brecht (1898–1956) employing alienation effects to distance the audience from the action. The Common Man was intended to act as a bridge between the play and the audience, though the role may have been misunderstood.

NOTES AND GLOSSARY:

Henry . . . who had all the physical and mental fortitude to endure a lifetime of gratified greeds: Henry had greedy ideas, such as making himself head of the Church of England, and physical passions—shown by his having numerous wives and mistresses. The phrase suggests that Henry needed to be very strong to live such a sensual life, and that he had strength of both mind and body

the monstrous baby whom none dared gainsay: Henry behaved like a spoiled child, but nobody dared to contradict him

an archetype: an original model, a prototype (OED)—in this case Henry is a symbol of the 'baser nature' present in all of us

vicariously indulged: vicarious means filling someone else's place. Bolt means that we can watch King Henry and derive pleasure from his greedy behaviour

a satisfying and disgraceful crash: although Henry's treatment of the abbey churches was pleasing to him, he was very wrong to act as he did

null: having no legal force

Vicar of God: one of the titles of the Pope, as head of the Roman Catholic Church

a sort of long drawn usurpation: usurpation means taking someone's name or title illegally. For many years the Pope (who is really only the Bishop of Rome) had falsely claimed the power to appoint all other bishops

the economy was very progressive, the religion was very reactionary:
England was becoming wealthier during the reign
of Henry VIII but religion was standing still
abstractions: ideas
we think of ourselves in the Third Person: we think of ourselves detach-
edly, as someone else
Stoic Philosopher, Christian Religious, Rational Gentleman: examples
of 'individual Man' as he has seen himself at differ-
ent times in history
get and spend if you can . . . get and spend you deserve it: typical attitudes
of 'the Right' (capitalism) and 'the Left' (socialism).
Bolt considers both misguided since they are entirely materialistic
we are thrown back by our society upon ourselves: we have no picture of
individual man to show where the individual
stands in relationship to society
an accelerating flight to the periphery: the periphery is the outer edge.
Bolt likens the plight of man in modern Western
society to the plight of certain modern European
and American cities, which often tend to be des-
erted after working hours
adamantine: unyielding
yield to the encroachment of his enemies: to encroach is to intrude. More
knew how far to let enemies intrude upon his own
personal ideas and beliefs
that final area where he located his self: Bolt has already said that More
had an 'adamantine', an impenetrably hard, sense
of his own self. This idea of each man having a
secret personal core with which other people must
not tamper is very significant in *A Man For All
Seasons*. Bolt speaks of the 'final' area because
there is so much that More is willing to share or to
give up, but finally he is driven to resist friends and
enemies alike when they try to make him do what
he believes is wrong
a person who could not be accused of any incapacity for life: More loved
life
perjury: the crime of telling lies in a court of law whilst
under oath
mumbo-jumbo: nonsense
equivocal: capable of meaning more than one thing, or evad-
ing the simple issue

inviolable: indestructible
something transcendental: something above and purer than human reason
paramount: most important
Albert Camus: (1913–1960). French writer and philosopher. One of his books, *La Chute*, is mentioned a few lines later
epoch: era, age
Who's Who: a book which lists notable people in society. Though no such book existed in More's day, all his guests would have been in it, had there been one
Holbein: (1497–1543) a German painter
Erasmus: (1466–1536) a brilliant Dutch scholar, and close friend of More
Colet: (1467–1519) an English scholar and Dean of St Paul's Cathedral, who founded St Paul's School in London. Also a friend of More
The New Learning: the learning of the Renaissance
he accepted and enjoyed his social context: he liked being famous, powerful and popular
aberration: a departure from normal behaviour
cosmos: the entire organised universe
mores: (*Latin*) morals and customs
frisson: (*French*) a shiver or shudder
empirical: that which can be discovered by experiment
tabus: things which are forbidden, not necessarily by logic
the social reference had been removed: Cromwell had taken away every normal law and custom of society
metaphors: a figure of speech in which one thing is spoken of as though it were another, for purposes of illustration and poetic expression
Brecht: Berthold Brecht (1898–1956), a German playwright
orthodox fourth-wall dramas: ordinarily in the theatre the actors occupy three walls of the stage—the 'fourth wall' is the front of the stage through which the audience see the action. Brecht and other modern dramatists have found different methods of presenting their work—sometimes using no scenery, or making the actors come out into the audience
Dutch courage: false courage obtained through artificial stimulants. Bolt suggests he got the courage to write this sort of play through the stimulus of history

more Royalist than the King: Bolt regards Brecht as the king of modern playwrights. Other authors are 'Royalists', or those who follow the King, and in their efforts to be like him, go further than the King himself

'Chalk Circle' (1943), **'Galileo'** (1937), **'Mother Courage'** (1938: three plays by Brecht

Rider Haggard: Sir Henry Rider Haggard (1856–1925), an English novelist, famous for his stories of exaggerated bravery and adventure

Eric Bentley: an influential modern critic of the theatre

reculer pour mieux sauter: (*French*) a phrase meaning 'to draw back in order to make a better leap'. Bentley argues that the alienation effect may make audiences draw back at first, but in the end it involves them more in the play

unicorn: a fabulous white animal with a horse's body, and a single straight horn on its forehead

the Common Man: Bolt means him to be 'common' in the sense that he is slightly vulgar, but also in that his ideas are common to all of us

tights: a theatrical costume. Strictly tights generally cover the body from waist down, though Bolt implies that the Common Man's close-fitting garment covers his entire body from neck down

the life of the mind in him is so abudant and debonair: Sir Thomas thinks a great deal, but this does not make him dull or slow. He is a very happy, lively man

ascetic: austere, stern. The opposite of 'abundant and debonair'

banked down: a fire is banked down when ashes are tipped on it to prevent it burning too fiercely. 'Banked down appetite' is therefore desire or ambition which smoulders but is not allowed to come into the open

hounded by self doubt to enter the world of affairs: Rich is really a scholar but he does not believe in himself and so thinks he wants a career in government

the minimal code of conventional duty: the least that a gentleman ought to do in any circumstances

coarsely fashioned: not elegant or ladylike, either in mind or dress

she worships society: she respects people who are above her socially

a reserved stillness which it is her father's care to mitigate: Margaret is shy and quiet. Sir Thomas appreciates this quality and protects Margaret from being misunderstood

megalomaniac: a mentally sick person with a false sense of power

the tremendous outgoing will of the Renaissance: at this time, with so many new discoveries being made, men came to have great faith in their own power

an all-consuming rectitude: his sense of what is right governs his life

the Holbein Henry: Holbein painted Henry's portrait when he was old and fat

he lacks personal religiosity: he is not a deeply devout man although he holds an important post in the Church

flattened Tudor arches: arches popular in building at this time

tapestry curtain: heavy embroidered cloth

incongruous: out of place, odd. The furniture is not realistic

---

Act 1: Prologue (pages 1–2)

The Common Man introduces the play. He proposes that the sixteenth century belongs to the Common Man, like all other centuries. Thus we are made aware that the play will hold a meaning for all of us. It will not be a story simply about things which happened five hundred years ago.

The Common Man puts on his costume as Steward for the first scene, preparing to step back into the action.

NOTES AND GLOSSARY:

(stage direction) property basket: stage properties are all the small articles used on stage, such as books, papers, wine cups, and the items of costume which the Common Man keeps in his basket

perverse: wilful, eccentric. The Common Man says it's very odd to start the play with such a plain character when there will be lots of other people in fine costumes who might do it better

speaking costumes: the costumes are 'speaking' because they tell us about the characters who wear them. The Common Man's costume, which at this moment is just a pair of black tights, is not a 'speaking' costume. It doesn't say anything about his part in the play

embroidered mouths: this continues the idea of 'speaking costumes'. The clothes worn by many of the people in the play will be embroidered, and this will tell us about the characters who wear them. It also suggests that, unlike the Common Man, those characters will speak embroidered or poetical language

prologue: a speech made before the action of the play begins

coloured propositions: continues the metaphor of clothing which runs through the whole prologue. The Common Man says that other characters could have made the first speech more interesting with elaborate language

closely woven liturgical stuff: extends the clothing metaphor still further. 'Liturgical' means connected with church ceremonies. Just as good cloth is closely woven, so will the speeches of the major characters be densely packed with meaning

the House of Lords: the upper chamber of Parliament, more concerned with ceremony than the House of Commons

to reduce Old Adam to the Common Man: the Common Man is now talking about himself and his costume. Adam was the first man created by God, and when first created was naked. He disobeyed God and in punishment was expelled from the Garden of Eden, after clothing himself in shame at his nakedness. The phrase 'Old Adam' has come to mean the sinful nature in all men. The Common Man is reminding us that he doesn't have a proper costume on yet, and also hints that we are all like him

a proposition of my own: he tells us his proposition over the page—the sixteenth century is the century of the Common Man

steward: the chief domestic servant in a great household

Act 1 Scene 1 (pages 2–9)

The Common Man, as Steward, introduces us to Sir Thomas More, his family and guests. We learn that Richard Rich badly wants More to find him a job. The unpopular Thomas Cromwell has become Cardinal Wolsey's secretary. More is called away from his dinner party to discuss the King's divorce with Wolsey.

NOTES AND GLOSSARY:

goblets: metal drinking cups

buy a man with suffering: Sir Thomas is 'interested' in this idea because he thinks Rich is proposing that some men actually want to suffer and enjoy being offered matyrdom. This would be a 'profound' or subtle notion

Machiavelli: Niccolo Machiavelli (1469–1527) an Italian writer who suggested that any course of action is acceptable if successful. Machiavelli's ideas were feared as they seem to argue that the State can behave immorally in the name of administrative convenience

you should go back to Cambridge: More thinks Rich should go back to university where he really belongs, and not try meddling in politics

the Cardinal: Thomas Wolsey (*c*.1475–1530), created cardinal in 1575

outer doorman, inner doorman, chamberlain: servants in a great household. To meet a powerful man like Wolsey you had to get past all sorts of officials, and often bribe them

he mistook me for someone: Rich does not say 'mistook me for someone *else*'. Norfolk dislikes Rich so much that he doesn't seem to recognise him as a human being at all!

a friend of Sir Thomas: the idea of friendship is very significant in the play. For Rich friends are people who can help you. For More the word has a higher meaning

office: position in the government

the Dean of St Paul's: John Colet (1467–1519). The post as schoolmaster has no appeal for the ambitious Rich

the Court of Requests: one of the law courts. More had been a judge in this court

in office they offer you all sorts of things: everybody in the government is offered bribes

I was commanded into office: More was ordered by Wolsey and by the King to accept high positions

he stooped from the clouds: Norfolk continues a conversation which began offstage. He claims that his hawk swooped down from out of a cloud. This would be very surprising, as normally a hawk had to be able to see its victim before pouncing on it

Meg: an affectionate form of the name Margaret

(stage direction) soapy: in a flattering or sentimental manner

falcon: a kind of hawk

a real falcon don't care: Norfolk says 'don't' rather than 'does not'. This easy-going way of speech establishes the sort of person he is

the very first cast: the huntsman carried his falcon hooded on his wrist. When he wished it to fly, he removed the blindfold and threw the bird into the air, or 'cast' it

Aristotle:	a Greek philosopher (384–322 BC)
Act of God:	any natural force which is beyond man's control, such as an earthquake or a tempest
heron:	a large marsh bird
God's Body:	Lady Alice swears here. At this time ladies were not supposed to use oaths. Her oath helps establish her forthright character
City Wife:	a merchant's wife. Alice is a snob and doesn't wish to be mistaken for someone from a lower order of society
very practical:	Margaret accepts that Machiavelli's ideas are workable ones, but implies that they may not be very moral
a farrier's son:	a farrier is a blacksmith. Cromwell was from the lower classes, and Lady Alice disapproves

the Cardinal is a butcher's son: Wolsey was said to be the son of a butcher

It'll be up quick and down quick with Master Cromwell: Alice predicts that a man like Cromwell who has pushed his way quickly up to the top will soon be pushed down again

the Queen's business: the divorce

is there a boat?: to get from Chelsea to Richmond More will travel *up* the River Thames. A few lines later Norfolk makes it clear that he is going to London *down* stream. More's is a difficult journey, while Norfolk will be going the easy way. This is not only true in fact, but is a metaphor of the way the two men will be driven to act in the course of the play. It is an example of the water imagery about which Bolt talks in the Preface

I don't recommend him but I point him out: though More doesn't think Rich is fit for high office, he does the best he can for him

the New Inn: lawyers were trained at the Inns of Court in London. Both More and Rich had been at the New Inn

Hounslow: now a built-up suburb of London, though at this time it was an open area of marshland and very suitable for hawking

That's where the Cardinal crushed his bum: apparently Wolsey had been riding at Hounslow, and had fallen from his horse, much to Norfolk's delight

Act 1 Scene 2 (pages 10-13)

Cardinal Wolsey tries to make More give his opinion on the divorce. He threatens, appeals to More's sense of morality, to his reason, to his political loyalty, and indeed to anything which might make More commit himself. But More is too artful to be caught, and he avoids giving a direct answer.

NOTES AND GLOSSARY:

(Puts cloth with papers, ink, etc., on table.): notice how the Common Man brings about the change of scene. We are no longer at More's house in Chelsea, but have moved to the Cardinal's office at Richmond

Latin dispatch: official letter, written in Latin

moral squint: a squint is a defect in the eye which makes things look crooked. Wolsey is suggesting that More is so moral that he can't see ordinary issues clearly

don't frivel: don't beat about the bush, don't avoid the issue

There are precedents: in law a precedent is an example of something which has happened before, and which therefore might possibly happen again. Wolsey suggests that prayer won't bring the King a son. More replies that such things have happened, and so might happen to the King

A dispensation was given: the Pope made a special ruling which allowed King Henry to marry Catherine, even though she was his brother's widow.

Yorkist Wars: the Wars of the Roses

Stage direction (Extinguishes candle): this stage direction offers us a symbol; it means something more than just putting out the light on stage. Wolsey implies that Henry is like a lighted candle, and that this light will go out if he does not have a son. Then there will be darkness, because there will be another civil war. Notice that a few lines later More re-lights the candle, which indicates that he disagrees with Wolsey. His candle is a symbol of the power of prayer

Fisher, Suffolk: Thomas Fisher (1469-1535) was Bishop of Rochester. Like More, he refused to take the oath which King Henry tried to impose upon him. He was beheaded just three months before More himself—see Act 2 Scene 8, p.86, and Act 2 Scene 9, p.90.

The Earl of Suffolk (1485–1545) was King Henry's brother-in-law and a member of the Council

Act 1 Scene 3 (pages 13–16)

After his difficult interview with Wolsey, Sir Thomas is met by Signor Chapuys, the Ambassador of King Charles of Spain. Chapuys tries to find out Sir Thomas's opinion on the divorce, and what he said to Wolsey. We also meet Thomas Cromwell for the first time, and see the Common Man in yet another of his roles—that of Boatman.

NOTES AND GLOSSARY:

Have you a licence: it was illegal to ferry people on the river without a licence

multitudinous admirers: Cromwell emphasises the words to show that he doesn't really mean what he says

plain so far as the diplomatic decencies permit: typical politician's language. Plain only in so far as it suits his purpose, is what Chapuys means

a nod is as good as a wink to a blind horse: a proverb meaning that one way of finding out the truth is as good as another

Dominus vobiscum: (*Latin*) God be with you

spiritu tuo: More answers in Latin. The full answer would be '*et cum spiritu tuo*'—'and with your spirit', but More is abstracted and cuts the answer short

skiff: a small boat

fathom: a measure of distance on the water

silting up: getting blocked up with mud

Act 1 Scene 4 (pages 16–20)

After his two testing interviews, More is at home again. William Roper is in love with More's daughter Margaret, but Sir Thomas does not wish the young couple to marry. His wife Alice bustles on, determined to get him to bed with a hot drink after his exhausting time at Richmond. We learn that More might be made Chancellor if Wolsey falls from power.

NOTES AND GLOSSARY:

called to the Bar: qualified as a barrister, and therefore able to practice law

advocates: an advocate is a senior barrister

heretic: someone who refuses to believe in the teachings and practices of the Catholic Church

It's a shop: Luther wrote against the practice of allowing people to pay money in return for which the Church offered them forgiveness for their sins

Forgiveness by the florin! Joblots now in Germany!: these phrases refer to the same practice of selling pardons, or indulgences as they were called. A florin is a small coin. A joblot is a bargain made without examining the goods

And divorces: Roper suggests that the Church will also let people get divorced if they pay enough, and this of course brings up the subject of Henry's divorce

Antichrist: the early Christians had predicted the rise of a great opponent of Jesus Christ, called Antichrist. Because some believed that the Antichrist would be a priest, the word became a term of abuse for the Pope

Lutheran: a follower of Martin Luther

Chancellor: one of the most influential offices in the Government

levelling talk: Alice has just said that 'Great men get colds in the head just the same as commoners'. More jokingly replies that this is a revolutionary idea and Alice will be locked up in prison for saying such a thing

the Tower: the Tower of London, at this time a state prison

Interlude (page 20)

The Common Man reads from a book which tells us that Cardinal Wolsey is dead, and that More is now Chancellor.

NOTES AND GLOSSARY:

Professor Larcomb: an imaginary historian invented by Bolt as a spokesman of a modern point of view on Wolsey's death. The older view was that he died of a broken heart because the King turned against him. Wolsey had failed to arrange the divorce for Henry, and the King was so displeased that he accused Wolsey of high treason. Wolsey was deprived of his money and power, and later arrested. He died before he could be brought to the Tower, though he would undoubtedly have been beheaded had he survived long enough

pulmonary pneumonia: a disease of the lungs
wilful indifference to realities: More did not care about everyday political opinions. Had he done so he might have saved his life

---

Act 1 Scene 5 (pages 20–25)

Cromwell and Chapuys try to find out how much each other knows about Henry's divorce, and about More's opinions. Cromwell also tries to discover if Rich is still friendly with More. Chapuys, Cromwell and Rich all give the Steward money to tell them what Sir Thomas says and does with his family at home. None of them learns very much.

NOTES AND GLOSSARY:

(stage direction) as one making an effort of memory: Cromwell pretends not to remember what Rich does for a living, thereby making him feel angry and ashamed

The King's ear: a very apt description of Cromwell, always listening, intruding, trying to learn secrets

deprecating: modest. In this case, false modesty

the constitution: Englishmen pride themselves on their democratic form of government—'the constitution'. Cromwell suggests, however, that this is only a farce, and that the real government is in the hands of people like himself who get on and do things, while the constitution goes on its own way. (It is, in the United Kingdom, an unwritten constitution, unlike that of, say, the United States of America)

the 'Great Harry': a ship which was partly designed by King Henry

a pilot's whistle: the pilot is responsible for steering a ship when in dangerous waters. He gives commands on a whistle

Lent: a period in the Christian year when people fast, or deliberately go without things they like

confession: Catholics are expected to go to their priest at regular intervals and confess their sins

parish priest: Note that Sir Thomas does not go to a fashionable confessor. Being a simple man, he goes to the humble priest at the nearest church

Dominican: a member of the particular group of clergy founded by St Dominic (1170–1221) who was canonised in 1234

bilked: cheated

Act 1 Scene 6 (pages 25-41)

The King is coming to visit More, but Sir Thomas is at confession and cannot be found. Henry arrives and everyone tries to be polite to him. Although he is supposed to have come for dinner, Henry shows that he has really come to make More help him to get his divorce. He tries every argument he knows to get the right answer, and when he fails, leaves without dining. After he leaves, first Roper, then Rich, arrive.

Roper is still pestering to marry Margaret. Rich reports that Cromwell is collecting information about the Chancellor and offers to help Sir Thomas to avoid trouble if he will find Rich a job. More refuses; Rich leaves disappointed, and his family warn More that this might drive Rich into collaboration with Cromwell. They want him arrested. More refuses since Rich has not yet done anything illegal.

NOTES AND GLOSSARY:
plainsong: a chant used in church services
cassock: a clergyman's robe
Vespers: evening service in the church
clerk: a humble priest
dowdy: shabby
hose: laced breeches worn by men at this time
cloth of gold: a rich fabric in which gold thread is woven with silk
Antiquone modo, etc.: the translation of the Latin is given underneath in the text. 'Oxford Latin' was that taught at the University, which was rather different from Latin as used in ancient Rome
a wrestler's leg: Norfolk is stout, and not as shapely as the King. He is built like a fighter, not a dancer
your Grace's Book: In the year 1521 King Henry had written a book called *Assertio Septem Sacrementorum* (a defence of the seven sacraments). This book defended the Catholic Church against the attacks of Martin Luther. The Pope rewarded Henry by giving him the title 'Fidei Defensor' (defender of the Faith). A sacrament is a religious ceremony. The seven sacraments referred to in Henry's book were: baptism, communion, confirmation, confession, holy orders, matrimony, and extreme unction. Luther had argued that many of these didn't matter. This book was of course written before Henry quarrelled with the Pope over his divorce

I brought them with me: Henry brought his musicians with him—even on a surprise visit to dinner! He was a capable musician and some of his music survives to this day

a licentious mob: an unruly or immoral crowd. Henry suggests that the quiet life More has in his garden at Chelsea is preferable to the bustle of the royal court

Dogget's Bank, Tilbury Roads: places on the River Thames

the very wick of my heart: a wick is the fabric which burns at the centre of a candle or an oil lamp

the Great Seal: the Lord Chancellor's badge of office

magnolia: an exotic flower

I stand in peril of my soul: I have committed a great sin, for which I shall be punished by God. Henry refers to his marriage with Catherine of course

ambiguous: not clear in its meaning

Holy See: the court of the Pope in Rome

It was a sin . . . I have no son: Leviticus warned that marriages like Henry's would produce no male children. (See notes on the divorce, pages 6–7)

I have a daughter: Mary Tudor (1516–58)

St Peter: Catholic tradition has it that he was the first Bishop of Rome and the first Pope

because you are honest: this shows how influential More was. If he would agree to the divorce, so would other people, because they trusted More

that air: one of Henry's own tunes which is being played

I expect I'll bellow for you: Henry is going to sing after dinner

Your conscience is your own affair; but you are my Chancellor: Henry is being unfair. Though he admits More has a right to his own opinion, he is an influential person and may not adhere to that opinion if it contradicts Henry's

Princes of the Church: many churchmen were so powerful that they seemed like princes. Henry himself suggests that there will only be one prince in his land—himself!

The Bishop of Rome with the Emperor's knife to his throat: in 1527 the King of Spain had taken the Pope prisoner and occupied Rome. Hence Henry feels that the Pope will have to do exactly as King Charles wishes, and will of course refuse the divorce

I was forgetting the tide: Henry uses this as an excuse to leave when More won't help over the divorce

nice: particular, scrupulous

Lady Anne:	Anne Boleyn (*c*.1507–36)
soupçon:	(*French*) a very small quantity
simple supper:	More is being ironic. The meal prepared for the King would be far from simple

I've got an inconvenient conscience: Roper talks a lot about conscience. This doesn't prevent him changing his opinions at suitable moments. His attitude to conscience is meant to contrast with that of More

Joshua's trumpet: Joshua was a prophet in the Old Testament. The Book of Joshua 6:20, tells how the priests in Joshua's army marched round the walls of Jericho blowing their trumpets and the city walls fell down. The idea is that when Roper talks so loudly of his conscience, Margaret's resistance is beaten as flat flat as the city walls

if you stand on your office: if you insist on reminding me of your official position

sophistication: Here Roper is suggesting that More is being evasive to the point of intellectual dishonesty

he has jumped the gun: he has reached conclusions before the evidence is shown to him. An athlete 'jumps the gun' when he sets off in a race before the official signal to start

the thickets of the law: a thicket is a dense tangle of undergrowth in a wood. Hence it means here a point of law which is difficult to get round

a forester:	someone who works in woodlands
the golden calf:	in the Bible (Exodus 32:8) the Israelites made a golden calf and worshipped it instead of God. Hence a golden calf comes to mean anything to which false respect is paid
Moloch:	a heathen god in the Old Testament, noted for his cruelty
put about:	a phrase used by seamen, meaning 'to change direction'
sending him up:	mocking him
bridles:	makes a gesture of dislike

Act 1 Scene 7 (pages 41–46)

Cromwell finds an inn where he can talk to Rich undisturbed. As More's family feared, Rich has turned to Cromwell because Sir Thomas won't find him a job. Cromwell bribes Rich with the post of Collector of

Revenues for York Diocese. In return for this he wants information which he can use against Sir Thomas. He persuades Rich to tell him about the silver cup which he was given by More (see Act 1 Scene 1). Rich does this despite knowing that Cromwell may use this to incriminate Sir Thomas.

NOTES AND GLOSSARY:

The Loyal Subject: public houses usually have names, though the name of this inn is clearly ironic

Collector of Revenues; High Constable; Secretary to the Council: posts in the government

no ceremony, no courtship etc.: one of King Henry's favourite phrases (see pages 27 and 30)

lifelines: ropes with cork floats attached, which were kept along the river banks. If anyone fell into the river he could be thrown one of these lifelines to save him from drowning

the normal aim of administration: a speech which explains exactly how Cromwell's mind works. His ideas represent modern theories of government as opposed to the old-fashioned moral ideas of More

a strikingly corrupt old person: a rude way of talking about the head of the Catholic Church. It shows Cromwell's practical and very modern kind of mind

a litigant: someone involved in a lawsuit

Chancery: one of the courts of law

Act 2: Prologue (page 47)

The Common Man asks us to imagine that two and a half years have passed since the end of Act 1. England is no longer a Catholic country, but has established an independent church, of her own with King Henry at its head.

NOTES AND GLOSSARY:

a lot of water's flowed under the bridge: a long time has passed, and many things have changed

torrents of religious passion: canals of moderation: a torrent is a fast-flowing river. A canal contains water which is not moving. (See the notes on imagery in Part 3, pages 51-2

fastidious: fussy, careful

Act 2 Scene 1 (pages 47–57)

William Roper is determined to wear clothes which show that he is now a good Catholic, and opposes Henry's new church. More is waiting to hear whether the bishops will accept the situation. If they do he will resign as Chancellor. He warns Roper to be careful in what he says: 'remember you've a wife now' (p.49). This tells us that Roper and Margaret have married in the gap between Acts 1 and 2.

Chapuys visits More, wishing to discover what the Chancellor intends to do. More makes it clear that he will avoid trouble if possible. He has no desire to be put in prison. Chapuys reminds him that Catherine has now been divorced from the King. People would take More's resignation as a sign that the Chancellor thinks Henry is wrong, and Chapuys also hints that this might start a revolution against King Henry in the North of England, where many Catholics support Queen Catherine. If More acts according to his private conscience he may therefore do harm to his country.

Norfolk brings news that the bishops have given in to the King. Only Bishop Fisher refused. More removes his badge of office, showing that he will no longer be Chancellor, but he refuses to state his reasons to anyone but King Henry himself. Sir Thomas hopes he will now be left in peace, but his wife doesn't think this possible, because he is an influential man. She is afraid he will be made to say something about the divorce and the new Church, and will then be arrested. More warns his family that they must say nothing. If, like him, they keep silent, they will be safe.

More has to tell the Steward that he càn no longer pay his servants' wages, and Matthew opts to leave Sir Thomas's service.

NOTES AND GLOSSARY:

The Church of England, that finest flower of our Island genius for
compromise: the book from which the Common Man reads is made up by Bolt to represent the opinion which might be typical of 'the man in the street'—hence it is just the sort of book the Common Man *would* read. But we must not believe such a simple and favourable view. The plight of Sir Thomas More in Act 2 will show the Reformation in a less happy light

compromise: the English pride themselves on their ability to find middle-of-the-road answers to political problems

we are dealing with an age less fastidious than our own: the Common Man is being ironic again. He is boasting that in the present day we are more fussy than were people in the reign of Henry VIII. But when he mentions 'imprisonment without trial, even examination under torture' examples spring to mind of this still happening in the twentieth century. The Common Man also boasts that the Reformation was 'achieved not by bloodshed'. In fact many people were arrested and executed, More being one of them

Convocation: a general assembly of the clergy, who had been summoned to approve the Act of Supremacy. More resigned as Chancellor after Convocation agreed that Henry should be given power to make laws for the Church as well as for the State

so far as the law of God allows: More hopes to use this phrase to avoid making his opinion public

a legal quibble: an answer which avoids the simple truth by playing with words

Socrates: a Greek philosopher (469–399 BC) who was accused by the government of Athens of corrupting the youth. For this he was put to death. Socrates refused to try to escape, preferring to die as a martyr for his beliefs. More emphasises that, unlike Socrates, he does not wish to be a martyr

Cheapside: a busy district in the City of London

Dominus ... excellensis!: (*Latin*) 'God be with you, my children'. 'And with your spirit, your excellency'

that holy language: Roman Catholic services were conducted in Latin. Chapuys calls it holy, as Henry's reformed church was beginning to conduct services in English. The question he really asks is 'how long will there be any Catholic influence in this country?'. More evades this very skilfully

Yorkshire and Northumberland: predominantly Catholic counties in the north of England. An unsuccessful rebellion called The Pilgrimage of Grace was launched from here in 1536. Although the Common Man has said the Reformation was bloodless, over two hundred people were arrested and executed after this rebellion

knuckled under: given in

Bishop Fisher: like More, Fisher resisted Henry over the divorce and the new marriage. He too was executed

abandon practice: Alice means both 'give up your post' and 'behave in an innocent manner'

I'm not one of your hawks: Norfolk earlier praised his hawk for being reckless. (See page 5)

tenuous: weak

Apostolic Succession: the Catholic Church believes there is an un-broken line—'succession'—from the first Pope, St Peter, to the present day

I trust I make myself obscure: he doesn't want to make himself plain, which might be dangerous

old Church . . . new Church: the Church of Rome and the Church of England

border: the border between England and Scotland. The two countries were often at war and More feared the Scots would join the rebels in Yorkshire and Northumberland

Old Alliance: between France and Scotland. These two nations often joined together to threaten England

Dago: a discourteous name for a Spaniard, in this case Chapuys

make goslings in the ash: literally, to make childish pictures in the ash on the hearth with a stick. Hence Alice means 'will you be idle?'

shall I teach you to read?: few women could read at this time. The down-to-earth Alice doesn't want to learn!

You'd dance him to the Tower: the Bible says (2 Samuel: 6) that King David 'danced before the Lord with all his might' to show his love of God. Alice suggests that Roper would willingly allow More to show his love by becoming a martyr

I have made no statement: legally More is quite correct—he has been careful to say nothing incriminating, but Cromwell will ignore the law, so More's safety is not certain despite his silence

even-stevens: exactly equal

Act 2 Scene 2 (pages 57–62)

Cromwell thinks he can make More give an opinion about the new Church and the divorce, if he frightens him. He claims that More accepted bribes when he was a judge. He tries to use as evidence the silver cup which More gave Rich in Act 1 Scene 1. Norfolk is able to prove that Sir Thomas gave the cup away as soon as he discovered it was meant as a bribe, so he is not guilty. Cromwell decides to find a more successful way of involving Sir Thomas.

We learn that More's Steward is now going to work for Rich.

NOTES AND GLOSSARY:

crank: someone with odd opinions

during the period of his judicature: while he was a judge

Cato: a Roman judge (234–149 BC), famous for his honesty

this is a horse that won't run: a plan that won't work

The King particularly wishes you to be active: the phrase sounds polite and harmless, but Norfolk understands that unless he helps against Sir Thomas he will suffer

This isn't Spain: political and religious prisoners were often tortured and executed in Spain at this time. Cromwell suggests that England is different

a net with a finer mesh: a more careful plan

Act 2 Scene 3 (pages 62–66)

More receives a visit from Chapuys. King Charles of Spain has sent a letter praising More for resigning as Chancellor. More refuses the letter lest accepting it should compromise him. He is now very poor, and his family cannot afford fuel to keep warm. Despite this, he has refused to accept money from the Church. Cromwell sends for More to answer certain charges.

NOTES AND GLOSSARY:

bracken: fern-like plant used in poor households as fuel instead of wood

whimsy: fancy

the money from the bishops: knowing of More's poverty, the bishops gave him £4,000 for his writings against heresy. More is afraid to accept this money: it might be taken to mean that he sided with the Church and against the King

pragmatist: one who acts in a meddlesome manner, but also worldly and practical

the merest plumber: a mere tradesman—a clumsy lawyer

Act 2 Scene 4 (pages 66–79)

Cromwell tells More that the King is angry because More will not state that he is right; when More refuses, Cromwell accuses him of treasonable conversation with a woman who prophesied against the King. More is able to rebut this charge. Cromwell then argues that More wrote a book defending the Catholic Church. More answers that the King himself wrote that book. Finally Cromwell states that the King has declared More a traitor. For the moment he may go free, but Cromwell still seeks to incriminate him.

NOTES AND GLOSSARY:

the Universities, the Bishops . . . Parliament: Henry asked for an opinion on the legality of his marriage from all powerful bodies in Learning, Law, and Church. Most agreed he could be divorced

Holy Maid of Kent: a nun called Anne Barton, who suffered from fits in which she spoke against the King's divorce. More tried to make sure she had a fair trial. Cromwell now argues that More agreed with her, and therefore committed treason; but More has kept a record of his correspondence and can disprove Cromwell's claims

charge: although he began the scene by saying 'there are no charges', Cromwell now admits that there are

a book: in Act 1 Scene 6 Henry and More discuss this same book, the *Assertio Septem Sacrementorum*

Bishop of Rome: Cromwell is being rude in calling the Pope by this title. He hopes More will object, and insist he should say 'the Pope'. That would be an admission of the Pope's supreme authority

canon law: the law of the church

a man who raises the gale and then won't come out of the harbour: a man who starts things and then won't see them through

Act 2 Scene 5 (pages 70–74)

More advises Norfolk that it is dangerous to be friendly with him now. When Norfolk refuses to accept this, More deliberately picks a quarrel.

A new Act has gone through Parliament, concerning the King's marriage to Anne Boleyn, and everyone must take an oath in connection with this Act. More hurries home to study the details of the new Act.

NOTES AND GLOSSARY:

Is it as bad as that?: the boatmen are now afraid to be seen with More. They won't answer when he calls for a boat to take him home

between the upper and the nether millstones: corn used to be ground between two great circular stones. Being caught between the two millstones suggests a hopeless position. In this case the millstones are Cromwell and the King

you have a son: if Norfolk is found guilty of treason through his association with More, his son will forfeit the right to inherit his title

mutable . . . immutable: changeable and unchangeable, respectively

we're supposed to be the arrogant ones: Norfolk says aristocrats are supposed to be proud, but More is prouder still

splenetic: rash, hasty

Sermon on the Mount: in the Gospel of St Matthew, Chapters 5, 6 and 7, Christ preached on a mountainside, telling his disciples many truths about human nature

Thomas Aquinas: a religious thinker (1227–1274) famous for his detailed arguments

pedigree: a record of ancestors. Used in the breeding of animals to develop only the best specimens

our friendship was but sloth: the only reason we were friends was that we were too lazy to disagree

a bitch got over the wall: one of the females used for breeding escaped and mated with an undesirable animal. More suggests that this must be what happened to one of Norfolk's ancestors

a new Act: the Act of Succession

stand to our tackle: be prepared

spittle: courage

rack: an instrument of torture, which stretched the body of the victim tied to it

bit nearer the knuckle: a bit nearer the basic truth

Act 2 Scene 6 (pages 74–81)

Time has passed again. Sir Thomas is now in prison in the Tower of London. He has refused to swear to the Act of Succession. Cromwell, Norfolk, and the Archbishop of Canterbury try to make him say why he refuses the oath.

NOTES AND GLOSSARY:

Thomas Cranmer: (1498–1556) created Archbishop of Canterbury by Henry in 1533, because Henry could trust him to accept the divorce

adage: proverb

an envelope descends: this reminder to the audience of what happened to the characters in the play is an example of alienation effect

Of course I recognise them: More is still trying to avoid a final clash with the King. He even agrees that Queen Anne's children should be the King's heirs. This is a matter for Parliament, and does not affect More's religious conscience. But he still won't take the oath, and the Commission must discover why

preamble: the introduction to an Act of Parliament, giving a summary of the Act

no reply: Cranmer asks if More believes the marriage to Catherine was illegal. More cannot answer without revealing his own opinion, so his only defence is silence

insult: refusal to answer a question in a court of law might be seen as an insult to the law and so the King as head of the law

assumption: a guess. Norfolk says that if More refuses to answer, the court may guess what he is thinking. More replies, quite correctly, that law must be based on proof not guesswork

material: of serious importance

my goods are forfeit: when More was arrested all his possessions would be confiscated

for fellowship: for the sake of friendship

like a dockside bully: in a vulgar and obvious way

cross of vestment: the Archbishop's official robes include a garment with a woven cross

commodious: far-reaching

Attorney General for Wales: a legal post. Rich shows little tact in asking for it when Cromwell is so worried

if I bring about More's death I plant my own: Cromwell sees that he will be unpopular if he has to have More executed. This speech helps to make the injustice of More's trial less unbearable for us

ratchet: part of the mechanism for winding up the rack

Act 2 Scene 7 (pages 81–88)

More's family visit him in prison. They plead with him to take the oath, but he refuses.

NOTES AND GLOSSARY:

has Eve run out of apples: Eve tempted Adam in the Garden of Eden by offering him an apple from the tree which God had forbidden them to touch. Margaret is tempting her father with something he very much wants, but which he dare not take

the worst that they may do to me: More is frightened of the terrible death which awaits him. But he fears also to lose his soul if he takes the oath

the upper gallery: More is in one of the dungeons of the Tower of London; Fisher is in a room upstairs

(stage direction) flown: scenery is said to be flown when it is pulled up into the roof over the stage where the audience can no longer see it

Act 2 Scene 8 (pages 88–97)

More is tried for High Treason. He is able to refute Cromwell's charges until Rich deliberately lies: he says More denied the King's title to be head of the Church. As there are no other witnesses available More is found guilty and sentenced to death.

NOTES AND GLOSSARY:

canvas and rigging: ships' sails are made of canvas, a very heavy cloth; the rigging is the arrangement of ropes which control the sails. Cromwell means 'all the complicated machinery of the law'. His sudden change into verse at this moment alienates the audience from belief in this as a normal trial or court.

the galley-master's whip: slaves were chained in huge ships called galleys, where they were forced to pull on the oars. If they did not work hard enough they were whipped by the galley-master. Cromwell is boasting that, under English law, nobody is punished unjustly. The manner of his speech is so unusual for a law-court, that we are distanced from his remarks and see the irony of them

Hearts of Oak: the phrase originally used to describe British sailors, who were thought to be as tough as the wood from which their ships were made. The phrase then came to mean all Englishmen. Cromwell boasts that justice is impartial for everyone in the land. Since he has bribed Rich to give false evidence against More we again sense the irony of his words

Foreman of the Jury: the jury are the twelve citizens who hear the case and decide if the prisoner is guilty. The Foreman speaks on behalf of the other jurymen

quicksands: dangerous places

Hall of Westminster: part of the Royal Palace of Westminster; used at this time for political trials

forthink: change your mind

the late Bishop Fisher: notice Cromwell's callous way of telling More that Fisher is dead. The implicit threat makes a farce of any idea of justice

rigged: unfairly biassed

the Kingdom: the Kingdom of Heaven

betoken: have particular meaning

qui tacet consentire: More gives the meaning of this Latin phrase in the next line

construe: work out the meaning

like a bat in a Sunday School: blindly, and without learning anything

pedagogue: a boring teacher

he denied the title: More had been careful never to deny the King's claim to be Head of the Church in England. Rich has been bribed to tell this lie if all other means of getting a conviction against More should fail

Southwell and Palmer: More claims that these two men were present when he spoke with Rich. Their evidence would be crucial, but both witnesses have been removed

red dragon: the Welsh national emblem which Rich wears in his new office as Attorney General for Wales

(stage direction) flummoxed: confused

repugnant to: opposed to

Magna Carta: (*Latin*) literally, the Great Charter. This ancient document guaranteed the civil liberties of Englishmen. It promised the Church freedom from interference by the King. More argues that Henry has breached that freedom, hence breaking the most important legal code in the land

Coronation Oath: at the ceremony when he is crowned, every English King promises to preserve the freedom of the Church. Henry has broken this oath too

---

Act 2 Scene 9 (pages 97–99)

Sir Thomas More is executed by beheading.

NOTES AND GLOSSARY:

my master: Jesus Christ, whose servant More truly is

easel and gall: the Gospel of St Matthew 27:34, says that just before Christ died on the Cross 'they gave him vinegar to drink, mixed with gall'. Easel is another name for vinegar; gall is a violently bitter substance

---

The alternative endings to the play

Bolt wrote two different endings for the play. When first performed in London, it ended with a speech from the Common Man; this is given on p.101.

This ending seeks to leave the audience with a feeling of being at once alienated and involved. But the Common Man's message in this version is rather trite—'just don't make trouble'. The message of the play is too strong to be summed up by so simplistic a formula.

The ending from p.99 seems much more suggestive, without forcing any conclusions upon us. Throughout the play Cromwell and Chapuys have seemed to be on opposite sides. The removal of More, with his uncomfortable honesty, allows these old enemies to link arms and relax.

Part 3

Commentary

Type of play

A Man For All Seasons is an historical tragedy. This allows Bolt to select a plot and characters of known general interest. The arrangement of the story is easy, since the playwright follows events more or less as they really happened. There are, however, certain aspects of historical tragedy which call for special skill and judgement on the author's part.

A history play deals with a lengthy span of time and requires care in the selection and organisation of events. It is not easy to make a plot such as this run smoothly, or to persuade the audience that theatre time and real-life time are compatible. The play may seem to keep stopping and starting. Bolt has managed this problem admirably.

His first four scenes take place in the year 1526, and sweep us through one continuous passage of action from supper time one day to breakfast the next morning. This continuity reassures our sense of reality, and moves us into the main interest of the action.

The Common Man then tells us time has passed, and that the year is now 1530—the year in which Wolsey died. A week passes during the action of the next three scenes, but this is hardly noticed in the forward surge of events. The Common Man continues to act as bridge over time-gaps. The planning of the play with no physical breaks between scenes also helps us to accept the passage of time.

Tragedy tells the story of a great man, and leads to his death through actions which are not principally his own fault. A sense of great loss is experienced when the hero dies, but not pessimism, since the tragic death teaches us new things about courage and suffering.

Bolt fulfils these conditions in his choice of More as hero. This successful stateman, author, lawyer and saint has always commanded respect. He was not born with the usual advantages of a public figure, since he was from the middle classes not the aristocracy. He had to make his own way to power, but did it by entirely honest means.

He lived at a time when Europe and England were changing fast. The Reformation, the Renaissance, and a cultural and social revolution were in progress. The retention of his dignity and integrity in such a time of flux and pressure enhances our admiration for More.

Bolt has selected those aspects of More's character which will emphasise his status as tragic hero, principally those which show his concern for 'selfhood'. The subsidiary themes of justice, power, law and integrity also reflect on More's unique standing as a brave and honest man.

The history of More has been arranged into a pattern which gives meaning to these themes, and the language of the play, with its happy mixture of the real words uttered at the time and of made-up dialogue, add the final element to a most successful historical tragedy.

By asking 'what kind of play is *A Man For All Seasons*?' we move closer to the main question; 'how good is it?' We may begin by noticing that it works well on the stage. It has always been popular both with audiences and with actors. Some of the factors which make it a good play in practical terms are its memorable characters and well-written dialogue. Nearly every person in the play has a rewarding part to play and is vital to the plot. *A Man For All Seasons* is well-constructed, and makes excellent use of contrast to sustain audience interest. It provokes thought, and remains memorable for its ideas even when the stimulus of production is over.

Themes

Good literature does more than tell a story; it embodies important ideas. The characters should be created and organised to give shape to those ideas, whilst retaining their freshness as observations of recognisable human individuals. What, then, is *A Man For All Seasons* about?

The Preface helps us to discern the themes and ideas in the play. Here Bolt addresses us as readers, not as actors or play-goers. Even if we have never seen the work performed in theatre or cinema we can understand what the author is trying to say. The Preface suggests that the principal themes are selfhood, government, law, and integrity.

Selfhood

'Thomas More, as I wrote about him, became for me a man with an adamantine sense of his own self.' (Preface, p.xii). This quality is vital to Bolt. He believes that 'the paramount gift our thinkers, artists and for all I know, our men of science, should labour to get for us is a sense of selfhood.' (p.xiv).

In what ways is More a 'hero' of 'selfhood'? The idea embodies a deep sense of respect for the basic honesty which each man should find in his own heart and conscience. It is necessary to know oneself: More had an 'adamantine' sense of self-knowledge. It does not involve false self-respect. Often the hero of selfhood is a quiet, modest, and thought-ful person.

More knew 'where he began and left off' (p.xii). He had learned to give in gracefully to things which did not harm him morally, but he was unshakeable in his determination not to yield the final area of himself where was located his pride as a Christian and a Catholic.

He could tolerate the new Church, even the new Queen, provided he was not made to swear a solemn oath that he believed them to be right. Beyond that point he refused to budge, even though he knew he would be killed for his refusal. He had 'something in himself without which life was valueless' (p.xii). It was this 'something' which would be des-troyed if he took the oath, even to save his life, to gratify his earthly master King Henry, or to relieve his family from the anguish of sharing his suffering.

Early in the play Rich talks of every man having his price. If that were true, there would be no selfhood. The play shows that there is no price, either in favours or suffering, which can make More yield his spiritual integrity. Rich, Cromwell, Chapuys and Wolsey all think and deal in terms of worldly achievement. More's attitude offers a contrast. It is because he knows Rich lacks a sense of selfhood that he urges his return to the University; 'In office they offer you all sorts of things . . . Why not be a teacher? You'd be a fine teacher.' (p.4).

The hero of selfhood must be generous at giving, not just know what he can take and when:

> My master Thomas More would give anything to anyone. Some say that's good and some say that's bad, but I say he can't help it—and that's bad . . . because some day someone's going to ask him for some-thing that he wants to keep; and he'll be out of practice . . . (p.9)

So even the worldly Steward recognises dimly that More is a special kind of person, and that this quality may lead him into danger in the selfish circumstances of everyday life.

What More *does* wish to keep is, of course, this same selfhood. He explains to his wife after King Henry's visit to Chelsea: 'I neither could nor would rule my King. But there's a little . . . little area . . . where I must rule myself.' (p.35). More realises that Alice will be lonely, cold and hungry when he goes to prison. But not even the suffering of those he loves can blur the issue of selfhood. In this last area of our moral being we stand alone, without friends or family. More tells this to Norfolk:

> NORFOLK: . . . Thomas, look at those names. . . . You know those men! Can't you do what I did, and come with us, for fellowship?

MORE: And when we stand before God, and you are sent to Paradise for doing according to your conscience, and I am damned for not doing according to mine, will you come with me, for fellowship? (p.78)

The most moving statement about selfhood is that which More makes to Margaret:

> When a man takes an oath, Meg, he's holding his own self in his hands. Like water (*cups hands*) and if he opens his fingers *then* he needn't hope to find himself again. (p.83)

The same topic is discussed on pages xiii and xiv of the Preface, where an oath is considered a special token of selfhood:

> A man takes an oath only when he wants to commit himself quite exceptionally to the statement, when he wants to make an identity between the truth of it and his own virtue; he offers himself as a guarantee.

This is central to the meaning of Bolt's play, with its strong contrast of More losing his life but retaining his integrity for his refusal to take the oath, whilst Rich commits perjury and becomes politically powerful, at the expense of his immortal soul.

Selfhood is a personal matter, it affects each of us individually. The play, however, raises a number of related public and social issues. It deals with freedom, law, government, which are just as vital today as they were in More's lifetime. If More is a man for all seasons, then the problems in the play are for all times and seasons too.

Government

Government starts with rule over oneself, but equally involves the responsibilities of those who have to govern other people. How far does the individual owe obedience to whoever is in power? At what point may we disobey the decisions of our rulers? How far are those rulers justified in using any methods in order to achieve their ends? King Henry is More's sovereign, to whom he owes allegiance as a lawful subject. But Henry seems lacking in self-government. He is peremptory and changeable. His decisions are based on self-interest hopelessly mixed up with national concern. His failure to see the difference between moral necessities and administrative convenience contrasts sharply with More's superior vision. Cromwell represents a baser and more pragmatic attitude:

> ... its a matter of convenience, administrative convenience. The normal aim of administration is to keep steady this factor of convenience ... Our job as administrators is to make things as convenient as we can ... (pp.43–4)

People with a private sense of selfhood are accused of disloyalty when they refuse co-operation with this worldly but common factor of convenience. Such people do often suffer for their refusal, as Cromwell again makes clear:

> ... there are these man, you know—'upright', 'steadfast', men who want themselves to be the constant factor in the situation. Which of course they can't be. The situation rolls forward in any case. (p.45)

According to this very modern-sounding argument individuals don't matter. If government wishes something to happen, everyone must get out of the way or keep quiet. The name of Machiavelli is associated with the idea. Early in the play Rich argues that any man can be made to 'toe the line' if he is either bribed or frightened. This amounts to a belief that, as long as you are successful, the methods by which you achieve success do not matter.

The ways in which we are governed *should* matter, just as much as the ways in which we govern ourselves. Hence the themes of selfhood and government come together in the play.

Law

Bolt asks us to consider why some things are legal at one moment and against the law at others; why some matters are forbidden in all countries and at all times, whilst others are purely local. The Preface emphasises the bewildering number of *kinds* of law there may be in operation, but underlines the importance of recognising that human communities are and must be based on law:

> Law (extending from empirical traffic regulations, through the mutating laws of property, and on to the great tabus like incest and patricide) is the very pattern of society. More's trust in the law was his trust in society; his desperate sheltering beneath the forms of the law was his determination to remain within the shelter of society. Cromwell's contemptuous shattering of the forms of law by an unconcealed act of perjury showed how fragile for any individual is that shelter. (p.xv)

We see that this great believer in individuality needs the sanction and protection of the law. More's assumption is that if he abides by the law he is entitled to its protection even though he is unpopular with the rulers and administrators. Cromwell pushes the State into pure anarchy when he cheats at More's trial.

Law occupies a large part in *A Man For All Seasons*. More, Cromwell, Rich and Roper all earn their living from it. The King represents, or *should* represent, the supremacy of law over government, and Wolsey, as Chancellor and Cardinal, embodies the conjunction of civil and ecclesiastical law. Of all these, More alone seems aware of the morality which should control the exercise of law in the community.

Structure of the play

A Man For All Seasons is a meticulously constructed play. Its two acts clearly divide the fortunes of More into the rising and the falling phases necessary for balance in a tragedy. The scenes within each act offer variety between public and domestic interest, and counter-balance each other. Bolt has achieved a fine balance between action and talking, between public decisions and private deeds, and between cause and effect of the issues at stake.

He is careful to introduce some scenes where More does not appear. Thus he is able to shift the focus, and reveal the minds of the people who are in opposition to the hero of the play. Cromwell is the centre of attention in three scenes, for instance. His brutal pragmatism makes a sharp contrast with More's generosity and gentleness.

The balance between action and dialogue is well struck. The theatre allows for little physical action to take place before the audience, but *A Man For All Seasons* manages to persuade us that a busy and active life is going on. The description of Norfolk's hunting party, mention of King Henry's fine new ship, and of possible revolution starting in the North of England are examples of this. The sense of everyday reality is sustained by such details as Alice seeing Roper riding off on her horse, More's family cutting bracken to keep warm, and the boatman discussing the injustice of the tariff for ferrying passengers up and down the busy river.

Public and private concerns are nicely proportioned in the play. The character of Roper reminds us that More is a family man, and has to worry about everyday details even while he is pondering great issues. Norfolk's passion for dogs and sport, Alice bustling the Chancellor of England to bed with a hot drink, and the Steward wishing rain water was beer, are all humanising touches which lend an air of reality and factuality to the plot.

The characters

Bolt uses his characters to illustrate parts of the overall meaning of the play, but he avoids making them stereotypes. More is a good man, but is capable of being harsh, angry, and unworldly. Although we cannot like Rich he is a subtle study of selfishness and greed, and we are made to understand the motives which give realism to his power-hungry and uncertain character. The characters have their own ways of expressing themselves, and are individualised by their manner of speech; Wolsey is coarse, Norfolk blunt, More urbane, and Cromwell cunning. The metaphors and the vocabulary of each character seem a vital part of his make-up.

The Common Man

Bolt describes him as 'Late middle age. He wears from head to foot black tights which delineate his pot-bellied figure. His face is crafty, loosely benevolent, its best expression that of base humour' (p.xxiii). We are told that he was 'intended to draw the audience into the play' (p.xviii).

When we first see him he wears only tights, which is surprising at the beginning of a history play, where usually the costumes are a striking feature. The Common Man is demonstrably the bridge between illusion and reality, between audience and story. His age and figure suggest he is very much the ordinary man-in-the-street. The multiplicity of parts he plays makes it difficult to talk of his character as such, but his earthy and selfish humour, and his sense of self-preservation are common to all his roles.

He reminds us that ordinary people play a part in history, however unassuming their role may seem. And in the last resort it is the Common Man who is forced to act as jury and then as executioner. We know More is innocent but, in the same position as the Common Man, we are meant to recognise that we too would have said 'guilty'.

Yet the author says 'I . . . meant him to be attractive, and his philosophy to be impregnable' (p.xviii), and in a way he is. He has two sets of values: knowing he *ought* to be loyal to More, to refuse bribes, and to decline the task of executioner, we yet sympathise with the pragmatic sense of self-preservation which brings him unscathed through the crises of the play. 'Better a live rat than a dead lion' is his way of putting it. If he lets More out of prison, he will be put in the cage in his place and where's the sense in that?

As we watch More suffering for his beliefs we know there is a finer state of being than that of which the Common Man is capable. This suggests he is also 'common' in the other sense of the word; he is slightly coarse, vulgar, insensitive.

His dramatic function as bridge between play and audience is underlined by the fact that he alone talks directly to us. Setting the scene, and providing linking information, he reassures us that the gap between Renaissance and modern life can be readily crossed. His speech patterns and vocabulary are familiar, colloquial and easy-going.

Sir Thomas More

Although we feel, in the presence of More, that we are with a man superior to ourselves, we are not put off by him. He has many humanising touches. He likes other people, and shows many different ways of liking and loving. More, for instance, has a touching regard for his Steward, and is genuinely sorry when he loses Matthew. He is therefore a good master, who rules his affairs by love and trust. The contrast is with King Henry, who is secular master of all the other characters, but who rules through fear and distrust. Wolsey, Norfolk and Cromwell all stand in dread of Henry.

Cromwell treats Rich with unconcealed contempt, but More is patient and understanding with him. He can see that Rich is greedy and unstable, but still tries to be just and helpful as far as his own integrity will allow. Knowing Rich to be unfit for government, More attempts to persuade him back to the honourable but unostentatious post of schoolmaster. More's judgement and his tact are in evidence here.

More shows another kind of love for his daughter Meg. He respects her intelligence, and she is his friend as well as his daughter. The moment when they part at the foot of the scaffold is deeply moving, for in losing Margaret we know More is losing something he values both in worldly pleasure and in intellectual challenge. His love for Meg is revealed in the private jokes and allusions they share.

Another kind of tact and gentleness comes out in More's dealings with Alice. Though he often seems to take her for granted, almost to ignore her, it is Alice of whom he shows most fear when he is in the Tower. Bolt has stuck closely to history here, for Alice was More's second wife, and was comparatively unintellectual and humble in her attitudes. She was an excellent housekeeper, but lacked a sense of subtlety. Plain, simple Alice confesses that she can see no reason why her husband should be unable to take the oath, and her massive common sense shakes More. His love for her is a love of all the good simple things which enrich everyday life. Bolt shows great sensitivity in making clear to us that More, the martyr and saint, loved custards, wine, and good housekeeping.

Even with people he dislikes, More is a perfect gentleman. He treats Wolsey with the respect due to his high office, and tolerates Chapuys with something approaching amusement.

Though love and respect are the basis of his nature, he has other qualities. He is a witty man, master of both conversation and ideas. None of his adversaries can trick him into compromising statements, though they all try. He takes pride in his wit:

God made the *angels* to show him splendour—as he made animals for innocence and plants for their simplicity. But Man he made to serve him wittily, in the tangle of his mind! (p.74)

More is scrupulously honest. He tries to protect Meg from marrying Roper, despite her love for him, since he doubts Roper's stability and judgement. And despite his love and respect for the King he refuses Henry's pleas for his assistance, though the anguish of this decision makes him 'cover his face' (p.34).

He retains his sense of humour even in prison and on the way to execution. Yet he can be magnificent when roused. His final statement of abhorrence for Henry's course of action, and his sad reproof of the perjured Roper both move us to admiration. It is very appropriate that Bolt chooses to call him 'a man for all seasons'.

Richard Rich

Rich is his own worst enemy; callow, brash and insensitive, he is fated always to reveal his worst side. At More's dinner party he quotes Machiavelli to impress, not realising that even More's daughter will have read him. His is the tragedy of a man with a gift which he cannot understand or appreciate. His horizon is bounded by worldly ambition, and when he is frustrated in achieving this he becomes foolishly bitter. Even the Steward despises him.

However, Bolt humanises him. He is poor, for he needs the silver cup to buy new clothes. He is possessed by desire for success in politics, but shows no aptitude for the subject, for he makes a complete mess of using the cup in evidence against More. His nature is too weak to withstand the alternate bullying and flattery of Cromwell.

The poverty of his mind is revealed in the bare and unexciting language he is given to speak. His conversation is not enlivened by allusive metaphor or by memorable cadence. Perhaps because he has made Rich's weakness so overwhelming, Bolt leaves us with a sense of pity

for the man. This is underlined by the sadness of More's final reproof:
'Why, Richard, it profits a man nothing to give his soul for the whole
world . . . But for Wales—!'

Norfolk

An aristocrat, Norfolk is so self-assured that he can afford to behave in
a very plebeian manner. He admits his own intellectual weakness with
cheerful frequency, yet shows insensitive contempt for the socially
inferior Rich. His bluff pride can be shattered by a threat of the King's
displeasure, and he drifts into accepting the necessity of attacking his
old friend More. Norfolk represents in the play those worldly qualities
which are fine until challenged by high moral necessity, and which then
collapse into helpless reliance on self-preservation. People like Norfolk
abound in real life, where their good-humour carries them along until a
crisis occurs. Then they always figure on the wrong side. Bolt sees this,
(as with the Common Man), as a matter of sad fact rather than as something to be outrightly condemned.

Norfolk's speech is distinguished by its blunt and earthy character.
His grammar is familiar rather than correct, and his mind shows as full
of dogs, horses, hawks. His easy-going and attractive speech patterns
show us that Bolt means us to sympathise with rather than condemn
him.

Alice More

Alice is the opposite of her husband; obtuse where he is finely strung,
blunt where he is urbane, and practical where he is unworldly. When
More is arrested she says 'I don't believe this had to happen'. All his
ideas of selfhood pass over her head. She is acutely aware that they lack
fuel, food and security. Yet More loves her sincerely if without ostenta-
tion. Indeed he seems to under-estimate her, since she shows jealousy of
her clever step-daughter, and craves words of reassurance: 'He said
nothing about hiding me you noticed! I suppose I've got too fat to
hide.' (p.40).

Alice, however, has power, the power of totally honest common
sense. She is roused when More invites her to remove his chain of office:

ALICE: Hell's fire—God's blood and body no! Sun and moon, master
More, you're taken for a wise man! Is this wisdom—to betray
your ability, abandon practice, forget your station and your
duty to your kin and behave like a printed book! (p.52)

This round manner of speech, typical of Alice, is very attractive. Her language is full of earthy and excellent vigour. She lends to the play a sense of warm immediacy, and finally rises to genuine dignity in adversity. Hers is one of the best written of all the subsidiary roles in the play.

Margaret More

More's daughter reflects qualities which we admire in Sir Thomas himself. She is sensitive, intelligent and witty. She serves a useful function in this play, where many of the principals are middle aged, because she becomes the centre of interest among the younger characters. As the object of Roper's admiration she lends the play a necessary variety in providing a love-interest. Also, because she is shown to be close to her father, she can be used in those moments of dialogue where question and answer are necessary to make things clear to the audience.

But for all her similarities with her father, Meg has a touch of worldliness which temporises her character. We never see any scenes of passion between her and Roper, and have to work out for ourselves why she loves him so much. And when More is in the Tower she is willing to take an oath to try to persuade him to give in.

Hence she represents a mid-point between More's altruism and Alice's worldly wisdom. A little of her father's verbal skill has rubbed off on her, as we see, (pp.83–4), when she argues with him. Finally, More's great love for Meg reminds us of the precious things he has to give up in refusing to yield to Cromwell.

Cardinal Wolsey

Wolsey appears only once, but leaves the impression of a powerful, gross and decadent figure. He commands More's wary respect, and for a good reason. He has great authority and few scruples about using it as need demands. He shows considerable skill in his attempts to make More agree with him. Their scene together consists of leading remarks by Wolsey, which More needs all his wit to avoid answering. Wolsey thinks and behaves entirely like a politician, never like the distinguished man of the Church which he is supposed to be. 'Come down to earth' he tells More, (p.12) and this sums him up. His image for Henry's visits to Anne Boleyn—'he's been to play in the muck again'—is deliberately gross, but is characteristic of his manner of thought. He refers to Anne as 'that thing out there', seeing her as a prime female animal.

He never mentions God, seems sceptical of the power of prayer, and scorns the notion that conscience may dictate the decisions of statesmen: 'Oh, your conscience is your own affair; but you're a statesman!' (p.12).

Authority appears to come easily to Wolsey. He does not have to eavesdrop, to insinuate or to bully, as Cromwell later does. Nor does Wolsey descend to the outrightly immoral methods of Cromwell. His attempts to persuade More are those of rational argument, not those of brutal threat. Hence he sheds a light on the later behaviour of Cromwell, making us see the 'King's ear' even more unfavourably.

Cromwell

Good plays present characters who show change during the course of the action. More, of course, develops. He is the centre of attention, and his mind can be seen evolving. There is a development in Cromwell too, though it is less subtle. At the beginning of the play he is just a name to us—mentioned at More's party, where nearly everyone clearly dislikes and fears him. The mention makes us eager to meet him, though at first he seems scarcely to warrant the fear he has roused. We first meet him as More leaves his interview with Wolsey. It is significant that Cromwell has managed to be in just the right place at the right time. He seems to represent unsleeping bureaucracy, having the petty rules of the river at his fingertips.

But as his power grows his net spreads wider and his interests become more insidious. Since he is utterly without refinement, sensitivity or conscience, he is the perfect man for the job of 'King's ear'. His horizons are bounded by the practical necessity of getting things done, and he will destroy anything which stands in his way. Cromwell is patient and painstaking, like any secret policeman; his efficiency depends upon the remorseless accumulation of scraps of information, which he uses as unscrupulously as need be.

More's poor respect for him both as human being and as lawyer may be warranted, but Cromwell cannot be ignored. He has abundant low cunning, as is evidenced by his handling of Rich whom he flatters and terrifies in just the right measure. He abuses words, as may be seen in his speech of silence (pp. 91–2), ignores morality and subverts justice. For all his diligence, he is a coarse and vulgar man, showing a baseness of mind which makes even Wolsey seem refined.

Chapuys

A static character, Chapuy's shows us the heartlessness of the professional diplomats in More's world. This function makes it unlikely that he would develop much in the play. He is urbane and dignified, but utterly lacking in human warmth. His face is a mask of official discretion, and his speech a series of ambiguities and official responses. He acts as an interesting contrast with Cromwell, the one being an aristocratic politician, the other a man from the lower classes. It is easy to see the vulgarity and cheapness of Cromwell, but Chapuys's honeyed phrases cover a mind just as cheap and tasteless. In the stronger of the play's alternative endings Cromwell and Chapuys link arms, and leave the stage together, smiling 'like men who know what the world is, and how to be comfortable in it'. The heroic sacrifice of More should make us understand how base is the knowledge and estimation of the world which these two represent.

Roper

Will Roper's display of his 'inconvenient conscience' (p.36), makes an almost humorous contrast with More's steadfast adherence to his principles. His changes of heart are not callous or self-interested, but they are naive and inexpedient. More understands him: 'Now let him think he's going *with* the current and he'll turn round and start swimming in the opposite direction.' More is alternately amused and exasperated by Roper's desire to flaunt his conscience on his sleeve. He illustrates a level of earnestness which is not present in any of the other characters. With Meg he provides the centre of interest for the domestic and romantic strands in the plot. More likes him even if he doesn't respect his judgement. It is his lack of political tact which makes him attractive as an impulsive and well-meaning suitor. As a lawyer he offers insights into some of the technical discussions necessary to the plot. But his most valuable function is as a contrast with Rich. Both are young, ambitious, having their way to find through the jungle of Tudor politics.

Rich sells out to the basest interests, but Roper quite cheerfully sticks to the out-of-fashion side of the argument, always retaining his own brand of integrity.

King Henry

The entire play concerns Henry's wishes and decisions. Though he only appears once, his presence can be felt behind everything which is said and done in the play.

He is a man of strong contrasts: he loves music, is genuinely fond of More, and is worried about his moral status. Yet he is capable of appointing a man like Cromwell to see through policies based on the most blatant self-interest. He breaks his promise to respect More's silence on the divorce issue and at times reveals a frightening arbitrariness.

Fear dominates the response of most people to Henry. Wolsey is nervous as he passes by, Norfolk and Alice fear his reaction if More is not present to welcome him to dinner, Cromwell knows that death is the price of failure in Henry's service. Bolt was right to call him, in the Preface, 'the monstrous baby whom none dared gainsay'. His power and influence are obvious, and it is wise of the author not to show too much of it directly on stage.

His one scene, however, is a highlight of the play. Many sides of his nature are shown. Grace, affability, romanticism underline his greeting of the More household and his talk of retiring to a quiet life. Yet tyranny lies under the anxiety with which the elder characters watch his conversation with Meg, however. He may fly into a rage if she innocently says or does anything to offend him. Pettiness of mind is shown in his jealousy of Meg's superior Latin, and misguided fervour in his concern about the state of his soul.

Bolt achieves this extraordinary range not only through the situations in which Henry takes part, but in his characteristic speech rhythms:

> No ceremony, Thomas, no ceremony! . . . A passing fancy—I happened to be on the river . . . (p.27)

> . . . it was villainy then! Yes villainy. I was right to break him: he was all pride, Thomas: a proud man; pride right through. (p.30)

His changes of tack are disconcerting, seeming to indicate a mind so wayward that it is almost deranged. His arbitrary use of power is childish but awesome, the more so as a shrewd judgement motivates his desire to be gratified. He represents one of Bolt's greatest pieces of character writing.

Imagery

Certain image patterns recur in *A Man For All Seasons* :

> 'As a figure for the superhuman context I took the largest, most alien, least formulated thing I know, the sea and water. . . . Society by contrast figures as dry land . . .' (p.xvi)

Government and freedom are aspects of the 'superhuman', parts of the eternal world of Past and Future, as is the problem of Man's selfhood. They contrast with the petty details of temporal and local laws. Imagery is thus used to give shape to the debate in the play.

The images appear natural, since the play is set along the river Thames. So when More says to the Boatman, 'The river looks very black tonight. They say it's silting up, is that so?' the remark provides local colour. But it also underlines the darkening fortunes of More's life. The Boatman's reply that there is a clear channel out in the middle illustrates the safety which the Common Man finds in conduct and opinion keeping him in the centre of opinion.

More uses both sets of images when he discusses the law with Roper:

> Let me draw your attention to a fact—I'm *not* God. The currents and eddies of right and wrong, which you find such plain sailing, I can't navigate, I'm no voyager. But in the thickets of the law, oh there I'm a forester. (p.39).

Such images are employed by most of the main characters. When Rich knows himself tempted to betray More he cries 'I'm adrift, help me' (p.38), as though he were a small boat being washed away. Cromwell sees More in similar terms: 'There's a man who raises the gale and won't come out of harbour'.

Sometimes stage effects are used. More, failing to get a boat home, sees this as a metaphor of his dangerous plight. Throughout the play lighting underlines the water imagery:

> the stage now patterns with webbed reflections thrown from brightly moonlit water . . . (p.13)

> From night it becomes morning, cold grey light from off the grey water . . . (p.81)

Such images make *A Man For All Seasons* a richer and more satisfying play.

The alienation effect

Alienation means making someone feel not at ease with a situation. The German playwright Brecht (1898–1956) employed it to remind audiences that they were sitting in a theatre. He did not want comfortable acceptance of his work as bourgeois realism. Thus he used little scenery, and that was representational rather than realistic. His actors addressed the audience directly, and mingled poetry and prose in an un-lifelike mode of speech. Messages and slogans were lowered onto the stage; nobody could mistake this for a depiction of real life. So with Bolt; there is little scenery in *A Man For All Seasons* :

> Hampton Court is hoisted out of sight, and other screens are lowered

one after the other, each masking the rest, bearing respectively sun-flowers, hollyhocks, roses, magnolias . . . the screens throw long shadows like the shadows of trees. (p.25)

Though this prevents us believing we are really in sixteenth century England it helps us concentrate on the *meaning* of things in the play.

As the scenery represents places instead of showing them exactly, so the costumes represent what people are, rather than intending to show specific attention to realism. The Common Man is the extreme example; he keeps changing his costume in full view of the audience.

In Act 2 Scene 9 Cromwell breaks into doggerel, unpoetic verse, whilst establishing that we are in a law court. The sense of strangeness, of near farce which this induces, is a part of a conscious use of linguistic alienation.

Summary

A Man For All Seasons is both tragedy and a history play. Its themes are selfhood, law, civil obedience and self-government.

The two act structure reflects the meaning of the play, and the well varied scenes sustain our interest in both characters and themes.

The characters themselves are so conceived and grouped that they are at once representational and realistic. The author has given characteristic speech patterns and images to each actor.

The play employs imagery contrasting water and dry land, to support its discussion of domestic and cosmic issues. The alienation effect holds us off from over-indulgence in involvement at a realistic level, but draws us into the ideas being presented.

Part 4

Hints for study

General

Try to enjoy your reading. Remember that enjoyment is increased by understanding, and you will then have a proper motive for close study of the text.

Also remember these Notes are *not* a substitute for thorough knowledge of the text. Unless you are properly familiar with the work you are studying you can never respond to it fully.

Preparing an answer

Follow this drill: read, stop, think, plan.

Read the question carefully. Make sure you know exactly what is being asked. Is the question in several parts? How do these relate to each other?

Stop for long enough to let the implications of the question sink in.

Think about the best use of your notes and quotations as they apply to this question. Which side of the argument do you support? How can you organise your ideas persuasively, clearly and logically?

Plan your answer on a sheet of rough paper. Jot down words, phrases, ideas which seem relevant to the subject of the essay. Then begin arranging these random thoughts into an essay pattern.

Your essay should have an introduction, stating your intentions, and giving your argument in brief. Then comes the main body of the essay. Separate paragraphs should deal with each point you wish to raise. A conclusion should round off the essay.

Keep your quotations short; usually two or three lines are sufficient to illustrate the point you are making.

Unless the examiner can read your writing all your effort will be wasted. Neat handwriting is an essential part of the presentation of your essay.

Try to plan your time so that equal attention is given to all the answers you are asked to write. If you find you have run short of time, submit a coherent plan of the missing material. This, however, should not be necessary. Aim for four competent answers rather than one long one and three sketchy pieces.

When you have finished writing, leave a few minutes to read through your work. The hurry and anxiety of an examination always leads to some silly errors. If you can get rid of these by re-reading your essays, you will save a number of marks. Accuracy of expression and grammar is a quality the examiner values.

Study notes

The kind of question you will be asked can be divided into various headings. Prepare your work under each of these, and you should be ready to face any possibility. The main areas to be covered are: character; language; structure; themes and images; kind of play; background.

Unless you have special knowledge of English Tudor history you should avoid the last of these categories, though you must master enough to understand *A Man For All Seasons* thoroughly.

Keep a notebook which summarises your ideas under each of the headings given above. For the heading 'kind of play' you might jot down notes as follows:

A Man For All Seasons : HISTORY AND TRAGEDY

HISTORY: popular type of plot; particular significance of Tudor period; story familiar to audience; wealth of attractive and contrasting characters.

TRAGEDY: deals with events of universal interest; leads to death of hero; leaves audience exalted not depressed; how is plot contrived to effect this?

OTHER NOTES: Bolt trained as historian; his knowledge of theatre; influence of Brecht on *A Man For All Seasons* as historical tragedy; function of the Common Man in giving tone and shape to the play.

Such notes should provide you with a skeleton, on which you could flesh out an essay answer about the type of play Bolt has written. As with all your study, you must develop your own ideas, not simply rely on books you have read. Each student should think for himself.

The section of your notebook headed 'Characters' might look like this:

Most characters in *A Man For All Seasons* taken from real life (only Chapuys's attendant and the Common Man are invented).

Treatment of historical characters: slight alterations to reality. Norfolk in the play less brutal than in life, Rich less powerful. More, by contrast, quite consistent with real life—Bolt even uses some of More's own words. (Act 2 Scene 8).

Contrasts of characters and groups: young/elderly; noble/common; weak/strong; fine/coarse. Purposes of contrast. Quotations for each.

Developing and static characters. Function of each type.

Notes on individuals:
> MORE: contrast of wisdom and innocence; adaptability; humour; courage; trust in law; belief in selfhood. Quotations for each.

Make a similar list for the qualities and vices of each character. Each person in the play has characteristic speech patterns. Find quotations to illustrate these, such as Henry's easy-going patronage when not roused: 'No courtship, no ceremony, be seated.' (p.30) Norfolk's blunt, worldly affability: 'You see, Alice—you're ignorant of the subject; a real falcon dont *care* where he's going.' (p.5)

Specimen questions and answers

Question 1: Analyse any one scene from *A Man For All Seasons,* to show its function in the play and to demonstrate Robert Bolt's skill as a dramatist.

The answer to Question 1 could be organised as follows:

PLAN: *Introduction.* Act 1 Scene 2 chosen; memorable character clash; discussion of vital themes; dramatic skill in construction of dialogue and situation.

> *Body of essay.* one paragraph on issues discussed—conscience, duty, loyalty, freedom; a paragraph on character contrast— Wolsey coarse and powerful, More refined and withdrawn; a paragraph on verbal battle; paragraphs describing conduct of the scene, with critical commentary.

> *Conclusion.* forensic skill of the scene; dramatic tension; effective organisation.

ESSAY:

Act 1 Scene 2 of *A Man For All Seasons* is a short but very effective and moving scene. It contains only two characters—Wolsey and More. The impact of the scene is made entirely through the force of the dialogue, since there is no physical action. This is the only time the audience sees Wolsey, yet an impression of the man, his office and his influence, remains with us through the play.

The scene also introduces the main political theme of the play. Wolsey has summoned More to discuss with him the King's divorce. He urgently needs More's co-operation, though Sir Thomas is known to be reluctant to commit himself on a topic he finds distasteful. Hence we gain insights into the hero's moral, political and aesthetic sensibility. These contrast with the earthy realism of Wolsey.

The scene raises the themes which are dealt with throughout the play; conscience, loyalty, duty and freedom. Wolsey appeals to each of these qualities in More, but is too worldly to understand that More judges by standards higher and more personal than his own.

Bolt, however, is too fine a craftsman to leave us feeling we are watching a static debate. The issues are not clear-cut. Wolsey has on his side a sense of practical urgency. Up to a point he is right to argue that a great nation cannot be run on prayer and faith. Wolsey's power is magnetic, and More is forced to fight hard to maintain his position of non-involvement.

This clash of will enlivens the scene. Realising he will not have More's open approval of his efforts to obtain a divorce, Wolsey seeks to trap Sir Thomas into a statement which can be used to draw him further in. The tension in the scene comes from the cut and thrust implicit in this verbal battle. More's task is complicated by his natural desire to remain calm and polite, however brutal or underhand Wolsey may be.

Though this is only the second scene of the play, we have already heard of Wolsey. Rich spoke of his outer doorman, his inner doorman, and his chamberlain, and we have seen More leaving the comfort of his dinner party to hurry off for his late-night interview with Wolsey at Hampton. Hence we greet the scene with a sense of expectation.

Wolsey begins by making More feel uncomfortable. Disregarding good manners, he ignores the visitor he has summoned, and continues with his writing. 'It's half past one. Where've you been?' is his curt and inaccurate greeting.

He thrusts a draft of the Latin dispatch at More, knowing that this vital document will draw Sir Thomas into debate on the divorce. More is politely evasive; 'It seems very well phrased, Your Grace.' His observation that the Council should see the dispatch draws a typical comment from the Chancellor; 'You're a constant regret to me, Thomas. If you could just see facts flat on, without that moral squint; with just a little more common sense, you could have been a statesman.'

Wolsey sets a series of verbal traps, arguing that the continuity of the

House of Tudor depends upon the divorce, that civil war may return if Henry has no son, and that More's public duty requires his co-operation in the divorce. To each point More makes an impeccably correct answer, without ever being drawn into committing himself.

The debate is reinforced by the symbolic gestures both men make in putting out and relighting the candle, and More sums up for us his private convictions in a phrase we should remember throughout the rest of the play:

> I believe, when statesmen forsake their private conscience for the sake of their public duties . . . they lead their country by a short route to chaos.

The scene ends with More having the last word by reminding Wolsey that he, a layman, has expressed opinions more befitting a cleric than Wolsey has himself. It is a polite and deft reply; it reminds us of More's essential probity as well as his wit.

Hence, whilst giving us information which is vital to our understanding of the play, Bolt has, in Act 1 Scene 2, written a scene which holds our attention by the force of its character writing, the excellence of its dialogue, and the complexity of its argument. The scene sums up most of the clashes of interest and personality which run throughout the play, though its absence of domestic interest also reminds us of that other side of More's nature which he prizes and struggles to preserve.

Question 2: Write an essay on the character and function of the Common Man.

The answer to Question 2 could be organised as follows:

PLAN: *Introduction.* the Common Man a Brechtian bridge between play and audience; the two senses of 'common'; various roles played —Steward, Boatman, Innkeeper etc.; each reinforces 'common' in both senses; characteristics are baseness, knowingness, waggish humour.

Body of essay. a paragraph on the Common Man being the only character to speak directly to audience, and why—links between history and present day, conveying of background information, racy informal tone; paragraphs on the two meanings of 'common' —implications of each—the doctrine of basic survival; paragraphs analysing each separate part played by the Common Man, with discussion of atmosphere in each (but don't let this become a boring 'tell-the-story' type of list); a paragraph on the two endings.

Conclusions. the Common Man principal creator of special atmospheres and effects in the play; structural bridge between realism and allegory; economic overlap of function and character achieved by Bolt.

ESSAY:

The Common Man is vital to the structure and the ideas of *A Man For All Seasons*. 'He is intended to draw the audience into the play not to thrust them off it', as Bolt says in the Preface, where he also suggests that the Common Man represents that which is common to all of us. The basic idea for such a figure was taken from the German playwright Bertold Brecht who, by having his actors speak directly to the audience, strove to remind people that they were witnessing a dramatic spectacle which demanded intellectual attention as well as imaginative participation. The Common Man serves precisely this function in *A Man For All Seasons*.

He plays several roles; Steward, Boatman, Innkeeper, Jailer, Foreman of the Jury, and Executioner. He also delivers the background information which is necessary to the progression of the plot but not easily conveyed from within the story. Each of his parts, though necessary to the play, might be unrewarding in itself. By giving them all to the same actor whilst making it clear that they are inter-linked, Bolt shapes one of the key figures in his play out of apparently minor bits and pieces from the fringe of his story.

Certain characteristics and mannerisms unite the parts played by the Common Man. His speech patterns are familiar, informal ones, full of contractions of the verbs, such as 'what'd' for 'what would'; he cites popular proverbs and sayings; and many of his rhetorical questions have a tone which nudges or cajoles the audience. His tone is one of base humour, expressing itself through a waggish appearance of modesty, and expansive affability. These elements offer a direct contrast with the highly serious tone necessary in many of the other characters. The Common Man also represents the exact antithesis of Sir Thomas More. Finally, he lends an air of actuality to the tone of the play, by making us feel we are drawn into the action with him.

Having chosen a Brechtian structure, Bolt needed a suitable character to carry the responsibility of bridging the distance between modern audience and historical setting. Unless he made all his actors address the audience directly, (which would impair the sense of historical authenticity), he needed someone who could speak credibly from outside the main Tudor context, but who retained proper links with the action. This the Common Man does very successfully. As representative of humanity at large he can address us familiarly, whilst as Steward or as Jailer he can sustain a part within the story of More's sufferings.

The Common Man is appropriately named. The Preface reminds us that 'common' has two meanings. On one hand it suggests that some elements of the character are shared by the audience. The other sense of the word is illustrated by the worldliness, the base cunning, and the moral weakness of the character.

As More stands for heroism and the noble doctrine of selfhood, so the Common Man represents the philosophy of survival at all costs. The audience sympathise with this up to a point, for they share the instinct for self-preservation, as expressed by the Jailer:

> I'd let him out if I could, but I can't. Not without taking up residence in there myself. And he's in there already, so what'd be the point? You know the old adage? 'Better a live rat than a dead lion', and that's about it. (Act 2 Scene 6)

A little later he excuses his baseness to More with the words, 'You understand my position, sir, there's nothing I can do; I'm a plain simple man and just want to keep out of trouble'. So much human response to suffering and moral anguish is made in these terms that we should feel some sympathy with the Common Man, whilst respecting the passion with which More responds when he cries out, 'Oh, Sweet Jesus! These plain, simple, men!'

This sense of being swayed by both sides of the argument through a clash of characters illustrates Bolt's tact as a playwright. He does not lecture us on the problem of moral integrity. He creates attractive and human characters who represent opposing points of view, and through them he leads us to make our own discoveries and decisions.

Each of the Common Man's roles adds to his side of the argument about the doctrine of survival. As Steward, for instance, almost his first action is to take a drink of More's after-dinner wine. Though this is dishonest and is symbolically representative of Matthew's code of behaviour, it is such a human action and is carried out with such confident bonhomie, that we are lulled into laughter and sympathy with this healthy relish for life's good things. When More shows that he realises that Matthew has had a swig at the wine there is no loss of dignity on either side:

MORE: The wine please, Matthew?
STEWARD: It's there, Sir Thomas.
MORE: (*looking into jug*): Is it good?
STEWARD: Bless you, sir, *I* don't know.
MORE: (*mildly*): Bless you too Matthew.

In this first scene Matthew is Steward to the audience as well as to More, for he ministers to our need for information by giving us brief sketches of each character who appears. He thus reinforces his function as bridge between sixteenth and twentieth centuries. Bolt sensibly lets him play this double role early in the play, thereby making us used to it. There is then no problem on any other occasion when the Common Man is called upon to step outside the story to address us.

His function as scene-shifter is illustrated at the end of Act 1 Scene 1. Simply by moving a few hand-props in full view of the audience he moves us from Chelsea to Hampton. He is chatting to us as he does this, so we accept his totally unrealistic actions as we take in his very shrewd and realistic words. He talks about More's unselfishness, forewarning that there must be something his master wants to hang on to. As we realise that More will retain his selfhood at all costs we can appreciate the dramatic irony of this speech. It is also possible to discern how totally unlike each other master and servant are. And as Matthew introduces the word 'common' into his speech—as he does into virtually all his asides—we recall his function as the Common Man.

As Boatman he reinforces the reality of the scene with his knowing chat about the river and its difficulties. Like all ordinary people he is worried about money, his family, and the unfairness of the petty rules which prevent him making an extra penny or two. But his very earthy and factual conversation underlines one of the play's principal strands of imagery. The dark river, silting up at its edges whilst a clear channel runs out in the main stream has a metaphorical application to his own easy life as contrasted with the lonely and dangerous course More must steer.

His last function is apparent when he dons a pair of spectacles to read to us from an imaginary history book, announcing the death of Wolsey. His book represents the bland, easy-going attitude to history which is commonly accepted. He takes its dogma at face value because that is the comfortable thing to do.

Act 1 Scene 5 shows a less congenial side of Matthew's nature. He accepts bribes from Cromwell, Chapuys and Rich in exchange for information about More's behaviour in the privacy of his own home. The audience will have mixed feelings; whilst his breach of trust is base and mercenary, his manner of handling his interrogators is so shrewd that we can only admire his wit. He excuses himself readily enough; 'The great thing's not to get out of your depth . . . What I can tell them's common knowledge . . .'

The Common Man's shrewdness is apparent as he spars with Cromwell in Act 1 Scene 7. His steady refusal to understand Cromwell is sensible. He is almost the only person in the play to make Cromwell angry because he has lost a verbal duel. Yet he is, of course, perfectly willing to lease his tavern for purposes of a conspiracy.

In Act 2 his social and moral standing declines. He accepts a foolishly benign and partial account of the Reformation. Then, when told by More that he may have to take a cut in wages, he quietens his sense of loyalty by talking himself into a belief that it is all a trick played on him by More. He argues that Sir Thomas will not miss him. We know this to be untrue, and so does Matthew, but he values money more than loyalty. Thus Bolt judiciously begins to withdraw our sympathy from the Common Man; our attention must increasingly be on the nobility of More in Act 2.

The Common Man is a highly pragmatic but efficient jailer, and a pliant Foreman of the Jury. He is again bribed to inform on More, but shrewdly sees that fifty guineas is too much; he is being drawn out of his depth. This brings out his base but efficient sense of self-preservation. 'I want no part of it. They can sort it out between them. I feel my deafness coming on.'

He is neither deaf nor blind to the necessity of bringing in the right verdict at More's trial however. His verdict of 'guilty' is manifestly unjust, though Bolt shows that the pressure on him is intolerable. To save his own skin he must do as Cromwell wishes.

His last part is that of Executioner, completing the downward cycle of his roles in the play. His are the last words we hear: 'Behold—the head—of a traitor!', symbolically spoken out of the darkness which follows the execution. In the original version he had a final address to the audience. Bolt wisely altered this, since the Common Man and the play itself reach their logical terminal point with those basely inappropriate words.

The Common Man, therefore, is the principal bridge between play and audience; he gives *A Man For All Seasons* its atmosphere balanced between realism and allegory. His easy-going speech patterns, with their familiar contractions and mannerisms reassure us of the permanancy of the situation we are watching across the time-gap and the theatrical distance of the play, and his base humour and canny sense of self-preservation make him at once attractive and deplorable. We recognise him as spokesman of our own less worthy selves and are thus made uncomfortable by the part common humanity takes in the destruction of the heroic More. He represents a triumph of Bolt's skill in character drawing and of his structural artistry.

Some further specimen questions

Questions on the characters

(*i*) Analyse the character of Richard Rich, and the part he plays in *A Man For All Seasons*.

(*ii*) Write an essay on any one of the female characters in the play.

(*iii*) Examine the relationship between More and the Duke of Norfolk.

(*iv*) Discuss the role of *either* Chapuys *or* William Roper.

Questions on the themes

(*i*) What does Robert Bolt mean by 'selfhood'? Show how this quality is present in Sir Thomas More.

(*ii*) Many of the characters in the play talk about conscience. Compare and contrast the attitudes of any two of them to this quality.

(*iii*) Discuss the theme of law in *A Man For All Seasons*.

(*iv*) Write an essay on the theme of ambition in the play.

Questions on the structure

(*i*) What advantages does *A Man For All Seasons* gain from having two Acts, and from having its scenes joined to each other without breaks in the action?

(*ii*) Consider Bolt's use of contrast in *A Man For All Seasons*.

(*iii*) Discuss Bolt's use of the Brechtian alienation effect.

(*iv*) There are alternative endings to *A Man For All Seasons*. Discuss the merits of each, say which you prefer, and why.

Questions on the language

(*i*) Compare and contrast the language of Sir Thomas More with that of *either* Cromwell *or* King Henry.

(*ii*) Bolt writes in his Preface that 'the main interest of the play . . . lay in its having a deliberately artificial, sometimes . . . almost farcical style'. Discuss the style of *A Man For All Seasons* in light of this remark.

(*iii*) Write on Bolt's use of imagery in *A Man For All Seasons*.

(*iv*) Discuss the 'beauty and form of language' in Bolt's play.

Part 5

Suggestions for further reading

The text

A Man For All Seasons was published in Heinemann Drama Library series, Heinemann Educational Books, London, 1961, and in French's Acting edition, Samuel French & Co. Ltd, London, 1961. The latter edition has two photographs of the original production, and a stage-plan.

Other editions have been published by Random House, Toronto, 1962, and Bellhaven Books, Toronto, 1963. The latter edition has notes and questions on the play.

It has also appeared in the Hereford Plays series, edited by E.R. Wood, Heinemann Educational Books, London, 1963. See *A Note on the Text* p.9.

In America the play has also been published by Vintage Books, New York, 1965.

Criticism

ANON: *Notes on Robert Bolt's A Man For All Seasons*, Methuen Educational Ltd, London, 1971.

Biography

HAYMAN, R.: *Robert Bolt*, Heinemann Educational Books, London, 1969. The playwright talks about himself and his work. Covers other plays as well as *A Man For All Seasons*.

Background

CHAMBERS, R.W.: *Thomas More*, Jonathan Cape, London, 1935. Rather heavy going, but a very thorough account of More's life.

CAVENDISH, WILLIAM and ROPER, WILLIAM: *Two Early Tudor Lives*, edited by R.S. Sylvester and D.P. Harding, Yale University Press, New Haven, 1962. Accounts of Wolsey and More, written by contemporaries who knew them personally. Roper is the William Roper of Bolt's play. These are not always easy reading, since they are written in old-fashioned English, but they give insights into the characters of both men, and offer a taste of the true flavour of the period.

The author of these notes

TONY BAREHAM lectures in English Studies at the New University of Ulster. Formerly Open Scholar in English at Lincoln College, Oxford, Dr Bareham has taught at the University of Rhodesia and the University of York. He is author of a critical study of George Crabbe, and a bibliography of the same poet. He has published articles on subjects ranging from Shakespeare to Malcolm Lowry. He is at present editing the diaries of the Irish Quaker writer Mary Leadbeater, and collecting a volume of essays on Anthony Trollope.

The first 250 titles

YORK HANDBOOKS

The first ten titles

YORK HANDBOOKS form a companion series to York Notes and are designed to meet the wider needs of students of English and related fields. Each volume is a compact study of a given subject area, written by an authority with experience in communicating the essential ideas to students of all levels.

AN INTRODUCTORY GUIDE TO ENGLISH LITERATURE
by MARTIN STEPHEN

PREPARING FOR EXAMINATIONS IN ENGLISH LITERATURE
by NEIL McEWAN

AN INTRODUCTION TO LITERARY CRITICISM
by RICHARD DUTTON

THE ENGLISH NOVEL
by IAN MILLIGAN

ENGLISH POETRY
by CLIVE T. PROBYN

STUDYING CHAUCER
by ELISABETH BREWER

STUDYING SHAKESPEARE
by MARTIN STEPHEN *and* PHILIP FRANKS

ENGLISH USAGE
by COLIN G. HEY

A DICTIONARY OF LITERARY TERMS
by MARTIN GRAY

READING THE SCREEN
An Introduction to Film Studies
by JOHN IZOD